DEDICATION

*This book is dedicated to the absolute love of my life,
Taisha Locke. Outside of the gift of salvation in Jesus Christ,
I have no greater blessing than my beautiful wife.
She brings me stability and support in ways I never could've
imagined. She is the greatest and most fervent prayer warrior that
I've ever met. I couldn't do what the Lord has called me to do
without her daily encouragement and steadfast spirit.*

*Tai, I love you. I adore you and I thank God for you every day.
My love for you is beyond comprehension.
Thank you for who you are and thank you for believing in me and
wisely pushing me in the direction of God's anointing.
I am more Kingdom-minded because of you.*

CONTENTS

FOREWORD
The Apostle Paul

Finally, my brethren, be strong in the Lord, and in the power of His might. Put on the whole armour of God, that ye may be able to stand against the wiles of the devil. For we wrestle not against flesh and blood, but against principalities, against powers, against the rulers of the darkness of this world, against spiritual wickedness in high places. Wherefore take unto you the whole armour of God, that ye may be able to withstand in the evil day, and having done all, to stand. Stand therefore, having your loins girt about with truth, and having on the breastplate of righteousness; And your feet shod with the preparation of the Gospel of peace; Above all, taking the shield of faith, wherewith ye shall be able to quench all the fiery darts of the wicked. And take the helmet of salvation, and the sword of the Spirit, which is the word of God: Praying always with all prayer and supplication in the Spirit, and watching thereunto with all perseverance and supplication for all saints; And for me, that utterance may be given unto me, that I may open my mouth boldly, to make known the mystery of the Gospel, For which I am an ambassador in bonds: that therein I may speak boldly, as I ought to speak. (*Ephesians 6:10-20*)

But I beseech you, that I may not be bold when I am present with that confidence, wherewith I think to be bold against some, which think of us as if we walked according to the flesh. For though we walk in the flesh, we do not war after the flesh: For the weapons of our warfare are not carnal, but mighty through God to the pulling down of strong holds; Casting down imaginations, and every high thing that exalteth itself against the knowledge of God, and bringing into captivity every thought to the obedience of Christ...
(2 Corinthians 10:2-5)

~ The Apostle Paul

INTRODUCTION

What you are about to read is not just a book, it's a burden. The following pages are the result of God downloading into my spirit, day after day, as I've watched some of the most unusual events in world history transpire right in front of us. No one can deny the fact that our culture is on a collision course with utter disaster. Everywhere we look there is confusion, devastation, and a spirit of deception that has captured the hearts of multitudes. Sadly, many within the Church have also fallen victim to a horrible spirit of deception. The Word of God is being disregarded and the philosophy of the age is being readily accepted, even in the local church.

A couple of months before writing this book I gathered our team and shared the intense spirit of urgency pressing on me to just write these downloads on paper and put them out there for anyone who felt led to read them. A little over a month ago I started the process and as you might imagine the intensity has only grown while we've been at it. We are living in a day when people and agendas are being exposed like never before, and the demonic forces controlling it all aren't very happy. So we decided that we were going to work around the clock (literally) to get this book of prophecy and persecution and preparation and proclamation into the hands of people that want to know the truth of God's Word for these days and want to know how to obey it.

We can no longer sit back and watch the enemy devour our families, churches, and communities. We must push back against this giant tidal wave of unrighteousness that is hammering us on every front. The Church of the living God needs a spirit of urgency and fervency like never before. We are living in the days that the

New Testament apostles wished they could have seen for themselves. We are watching the most compelling and mysterious Bible prophecies suddenly making sense as they come to life on a daily basis. There are a series of urgent messages in all this, and we all know it, so it's time to take the Lord seriously, once and for all. I wrote this book to do exactly that.

As you might have picked up from the title, *This Means War* was not produced to make you feel comfortable. This book is a call to action. I refuse to sit idly by while the "lukewarm" spirit overtakes the church in our culture. I refuse to allow this nation to be destroyed while the body of Christ is brought to ruin right along with it—not on my watch. I have reached a place in my life where it no longer matters what anyone calls me, as long as God Himself never calls me a coward. We are one election away from losing everything that we hold dear. We must stand now! We must speak out now! We must fight back now! We can no longer surrender through our silence. Our compromise is wrapped in our complacency, and the enemy has swiftly come to destroy the moral foundations of this nation and the very fabric of our society. This is a fight against everything evil and wicked in this world, and by all indications, this is a battle for the souls of humanity. This is a noble cause. This is a call to real repentance. This is a rallying of the troops in God's holy Army. This is our day. This is our time. This means something for the Kingdom. As a matter of fact, THIS MEANS WAR.

Part I: Prophecy

"Watch therefore: for ye know not what hour your Lord doth come. But know this, that if the goodman of the house had known in what watch the thief would come, he would have watched, and would not have suffered his house to be broken up. Therefore be ye also ready: for in such an hour as ye think not the Son of man cometh. Who then is a faithful and wise servant, whom his lord hath made ruler over his household, to give them meat in due season? Blessed is that servant, whom his lord when he cometh shall find so doing." ~Jesus

Matthew 24:42-46

1

The Coming Evil

Let's begin by discussing one of the most unusual passages in the Bible. If you've been studying the Word of God for a while you've probably become familiar with the urgent prophetic message Jesus delivers in this discourse. Before jumping in, I've got to confess a couple of things.

I want you to know that in twenty-eight years of preaching and teaching and writing about the Bible, I've studied it, I've mentioned it, I've quoted it, I've talked about it and I've sectionalized it, but I've never explored this particular passage in Matthew Chapter 24 the way I will here—mostly due to its heavy foreboding. It can without question be a bit scary.

If we take Jesus at His word, we all need to take this passage very seriously right now, especially considering all that awaits us. This particular passage has been known to confuse a lot of people, so I want to unwind it a little bit and ensure it doesn't trigger fear of anything but the Lord Himself. I wouldn't have stopped to write this if I didn't believe it will equip you and encourage you for the seasons that are just over the horizon.

No Slop Zone

It's my responsibility as a teacher of the Bible to feed the flock, not slop the hogs. There's a big difference. I'm not writing for the purpose of entertainment, but for the purpose of breaking down the Bible in a way that helps the reader see both its prophetic nature and its practical application. The Bible is real and alive and "up to date" this very moment. It is applicable to your life, to your home, to your marriage, and to your calling no matter what you believe or how you've lived in the past. I believe God has been speaking on a lot of different levels through various avenues and recent events, and all these centuries after its completion, the Bible is still preeminent among them. Through it all, I believe—for the most part—the people of God have been listening.

I believe you've been listening, and I think that's why you're reading this book. You're seeking something bigger and greater than who you are or what you are and you want to be ready for what God is preparing to do. I also realize that you might be giving this book a half-hearted spin because somebody recommended it, or maybe even because you hate my video messages or the imperfect messenger that I am—or both—and want to see if you can find more to hate.

Whatever the case, I want to challenge you to stick with me to the end. I can assure you that you won't be sorry that you read this book, even if you're committed to hating Greg Locke. Don't let a spirit of criticism or your opinion of me rob you of the reasons the Holy Ghost led you to reading this. Every relationship, good or bad, can teach you. We can learn from the worst of situations. We can even learn from people that we don't respect if we're teachable and recognize truth when we see it. In Psalm 143:10 David said, "Oh God teach me to do thy will." If we're going to be taught the will of God, then we are going to have to be teachable even when the stones cry out.

Opening Prayer

As we begin, please take a moment to pray these words with me. Father in heaven, we come to you in the name that is above every name, the name of Jesus Christ. We pray Father that through the messages in this book You will encourage our hearts and spark a renewed vision for tomorrow. Bless us Lord, bless Your Church, bless all people everywhere on this amazing planet. Thank you for the promise that you will overshadow us with the power of your presence, Father. Thank you for reminding us that greater is He that is in us than he that is in this world. He that is in this world is stirring up a lot of chaos and craziness and wickedness in these historic times, but You are bigger and more wonderful than all, You are the Author of all, and we trust in You alone, as we fear not what man and the forces of evil can do unto us. Bless the power of your Word today Father. Give us liberty, give us grace, as we offer this time to You. We thank You for what You're about to do... in the mighty name of Jesus, amen and amen.

The Olivet Discourse

Theologically speaking, Matthew Chapter 24 is one of the most daunting passages in the whole Bible and even more so among all Jesus Christ had to say during the three and one-half years of His ministry upon this earth. We often call Matthew Chapters 24 and 25 the *Olivet Discourse*, because the famous teaching was delivered from the Mount of Olives, just outside of Jerusalem.

Ninety-eight percent of everything Jesus talks about in Matthew Chapter 24 is of a prophetic nature, and it all deals with the seasons leading up to His return. If you can't see that Biblical prophecy is being fulfilled before our very eyes then you've had your head in the sand and you're not paying attention.

I'm not going to spend a lot of time ranting about the schemes of the enemy (my short videos serve that purpose), so I'll trust you're becoming increasingly aware as you lift up your head a little more each passing day. Again, I believe you've been listening and beginning to see more clearly. Now we all need to use both our brains and our Bibles to recognize that Jesus Christ is indeed coming again as the Bible says, and by all indications it will be well sooner than we think. In fact, Jesus said that it would be.

Lift up your eyes for your redemption draweth nigh, the days are getting short and the days are getting dark. Romans chapter one tells us "the whole creation groans for the return of

Jesus Christ," and all can hear these groans, even if they don't understand what it all means. Even the secular world knows that Jesus is getting ready to come again. They can sense it, and it shows through their desperate efforts to strike down anything and anyone who stands for Biblical principles. I know what the progressives say and I know what the far left and the socialist crowd says. They believe that—once they correct everything to fit their world view—it's just going to get better and better and better, and one day they're going to usher in a utopian society.

That is not what the Bible teaches. The Bible teaches that it's going to get worse and worse and worse, and people will become so disobedient and so diabolical and so dangerous that the only way it can be fixed is for Jesus to split the sky and come to take up His children. It's the only way we can rise above it. Jesus is coming again folks. Soon. Are we ready?

The Tribulation

Before diving in, let me put aside a couple of theological conjectures and arguments that I'm not going to get into in this short book. Regardless of where you stand regarding the timing or theological reality of the rapture, regardless of what you believe about when Jesus is coming again, it doesn't change the context of what is already being fulfilled in Matthew Chapter 24.

While most folks fall into three camps concerning His return and the rapture—pre-tribulation, mid-tribulation, or post-tribulation—I personally believe we'll have the unmerited blessing of a pre-tribulation rapture, praise God, with Jesus returning to claim His church before the tribulation actually begins. I don't find this to be a divisive topic, but some do, so I hope you don't let this issue distract you from the message if you're in another camp. As long as you believe Jesus is indeed returning to claim His Church at some point surrounding the tribulation, we're actually on the same side of the bigger debate. For those who have never discussed or considered the subject, let me share my thoughts in the briefest form. I base my "pre-trib" belief on the reality that the Bible says the tribulation is not for the Church but is a time of Jacob's trouble (Jeremiah 37). It's a time for the Israeli judgment, the rebirth of Zion, as the nation that rejected Him shall be born in a day (Isaiah 66:8). Likewise, in Romans Paul taught us that all who are born again in Christ have been delivered from the wrath to come, and Revelation 13 says that during the tribulation God pours out His wrath without measure, so I do not believe the bride of Christ is going to be here to suffer these days of wrath. I just don't. I'm not looking for the Antichrist, I'm looking for Jesus Christ.

In these days, everyone is asking, "Who is the Antichrist? What does he look like? Is he already alive?" I have absolutely no idea, but Bernie Sanders missed a great opportunity! There is no doubt about that, amen? If that comment made you nervous wait a few more paragraphs and you are really going to start squirming. It's good to laugh a bit up front because it can lessen the sting if I inadvertently take a jab at you along the way.

Millennial Reign

Regardless of whether you believe we're going to get rescued before, during, or after the tribulation, and no matter where you stand regarding the Lord's return, no one can deny we are already seeing prophetic events being fulfilled that are clearly in context with the second coming of Christ. I'm learning that a lot of church folks haven't been taught a thing about what to expect next, so let me remind you (or inform you) that Jesus is not coming to just snatch us away, but to return with us back to the earth and to rule and reign as our King for 1000 years, and we live on forever doing whatever He plans next.

Can you imagine that? Have you ever tried to imagine that? You should. Talk about an amazing time to be alive. And though we won't be discussing this "millennial reign" in this book, I want to make sure we all know what we are fighting for in a war Jesus already won for us. Now all we have to do is walk it out as He instructed. It's the most beautiful news imaginable for those of us who are saved and born again so I hope this book helps you embrace this season with the heart of a warrior and the enthusiasm of a child.

True believers from every generation receive eternal life with Christ on earth *and* in heaven. We'd better get ready because this exciting mysterious reality is coming to a town near you sometime in the near future. That being said, I'll admit I don't have any idea exactly when that will be, and I'm definitely not waiting around looking for signs to determine my beliefs or my obedience. I'm just looking for the Son of God. But I can't deny the reality of the massive signs that are being fulfilled around the world right this very moment. Jesus warns us not to be a generation that waits for signs before acting on the Word of God, but He definitely expects us to "discern the signs of the times" when they clearly appear as we're seeing today (Matthew 16:2-4).

When we talk about the last days, we'll often hear people say, "you people have been talking about the last days for an awful long time." Considering that the church has kept the faith for 2000 years, we at very least need to realize that we're that much closer than every generation before us.

2000 Years Later

Hebrews 1:2 says in the last days God will speak to us by His Son… by His Son… by His Son… whom He has appointed heir of all things. The last days literally started when Jesus ascended into heaven after His death and resurrection, so they've actually been unfolding ever since. And suddenly many communities and the cultures around us are rocking and reeling and burning to the ground and people are wondering, "where are the signs of His coming?" I see their dismissive comments in my social media channels all the time. They write, "*You funny-mentalists… you fuddy duddy loudmouth Christians… you've been spreading this fairytale and sipping that Kool-Aid for 2000 years.*"

Can I remind you that it took Jesus 4000 years to show up the first time? We are watching the Bible be fulfilled right before our very eyes. Not just every year, but EVERY WEEK in the United States and around the world. Jesus Christ is, without question, coming again and no one can know the day or the hour, make no mistake about that. It could even be tonight, no matter what men say. Let's get ready.

What Is Truth?

Culturally, it feels as if the world has been propelled 50 years into the prophetic narrative over the last six months. To put that into the socio-political context, the deconstruction of Christian influence in America has been the primary goal of globalist progressives over the past 50 years. Somehow this formerly impossible goal has been accomplished over a few short months during 2020, as mainstream media corruption and globalist misinformation hysteria has literally taken control of the minds of hundreds of millions of people.

We're living a world of lies and deception. Prompted by Jesus' statement that "everyone who is of the truth listens to my voice," the Roman Governor Pontius Pilate famously asked Jesus, "What is truth?" In retrospect, knowing Pilate was looking at "the truth" while condemning Him to death on the cross, that moment is proving more prophetic than we could ever have imagined just a few years ago. (John 18:38)

Regardless of where you stand, you will not be able to deny the theological implications of what I'm about to address, for we are watching it unfold on the movie screen of our lives in real time. Matthew 24:3 tells us that when Jesus sat upon the Mount of Olives, the disciples came unto Him loaded with questions about His second coming. I remind you these are the guys that walked with Him and talked with Him and saw Him perform miracles daily for more than three years, and yet they were still loaded with questions and concerns. They came unto him "privately" because what they wanted to ask was a little bit embarrassing, as it were. So they asked Jesus, "tell us, when shall these things be?"

Jesus had just predicted the fall of Jerusalem—a prophetic statement that was quickly fulfilled in AD 70, which was just a few decades later. The Roman army literally went into Jerusalem and stomped the temple to the ground, scattering the children of Israel to all corners of the known earth. Let me interject, the nation of Israel is already in the foundational phase—in this generation—of the building of that temple, which is a prophetic event that most theologians believe must come to pass before the entirety of Matthew 24 can be fulfilled.

You'd better believe they're doing all they can to restore the temple right this very second. Keeping all that in mind, let's return to the disciples' questions in verse 24:3, "Tell us, when shall these things be? and what shall be the sign of thy coming, and of the end of the world?" Many are asking these questions more today than ever.

Still a Long Way to Go

When we talk about the end of the world, let's be reminded that even if Jesus came this very millisecond, we'll still have up to seven years of tribulation on the earth, we'll still have the 1000 years of millennial reign, and we'll still have the battle of Armageddon that ushers in the end.

As detailed in Revelation Chapter 20, during this 1000 years the devil will in effect be imprisoned, yet even after a millennium of silent incarceration he will still be crazy enough to believe he can beat Jesus and destroy His bride, because—after all—that's all he exists for anymore. Thank God we all know how the story ends, as the devil is going to get whooped for all to see when Jesus opens his mouth and reveals a sharp two-edged sword that He'll use to smite the nations that stand in opposition to Him and His own.

In 2 Peter 3:10, the Bible tells us ..."the day of the Lord will come as a thief in the night; in which the heavens shall pass away with a great noise, and the elements shall melt with fervent heat, the earth also and the works that are therein shall be burned up."

The world is eventually going to be destroyed, and at that time God is going to create a new heaven and a new earth. For all this, if Jesus is your Lord and Savior, be encouraged, be very encouraged, but ready yourself for the spiritual war that is only just now beginning.

2

When Shall These Things Be?

And as he sat upon the mount of Olives, the disciples came unto him privately, saying, Tell us, when shall these things be? and what shall be the sign of thy coming, and of the end of the world? And Jesus answered and said unto them, Take heed that no man deceive you.

~ Matthew 24:3-4

The Lord spoke this world into existence, and He's going to speak this world out of existence. Though the end is still a long way away, today we're watching it gear up. It's a question every human considers at some point. As we see in Matthew 24, even the first disciples asked, "when shall it be?"

Jesus answered this question with unusual detail, and we're beginning to see it play out in our generation. Matthew recorded that "Jesus answered," so let me assure you it doesn't say "Greg answered." It doesn't say the Baptists or the *Episcolopians* (intentionally misspelled) or the charismatics or the Church of God or the Catholics or anybody else. It says, "JESUS answered!"

You can deny and hate the word of Greg all you want but you'd better not deny and hate the word of God. Jesus then answered and said unto them, "take heed that no man deceive you." Did you know that the dark spirit that is attacking the Church around the world today is the spirit of deception? There's a palpable atmosphere of deception among God's people these days, unlike anything that has ever plagued the Church. This is markedly different.

I used to wonder how in the world the Antichrist could ever sell the masses an evil bill of goods in the modern world. What sort of people would ever cooperate with him and believe in him? In these days of mass communications and mass global proliferation of Christian thought, what generation could ever believe such lies? Yet anytime we open Facebook we can see clearly that most sheep are believing whatever they're told by the mainstream media. Let no man deceive you!

Sometimes you've got to get your nose out of the news. Sometimes you've got to turn off Facebook and get your face in The Book. People are being deceived, people are being lied to, and people are literally having their lives destroyed because of a spirit of deception—politically, economically, materialistically, maritally, etc. You name the institution, and if you have eyes that see and ears that hear, you'll find deception hard at work, and religious circles are no exception. In fact, we've become the primary target. It appears they're comfortable with their degree of control over the masses so they're finally coming after us, and so far, they're winning on most fronts.

False Christs?

For many shall come in my name, saying, I am Christ; and shall deceive many.

~ *Matthew 24:5*

I could expand on the subject of deception in the Church for several chapters, but it's more important that we zero in on the reasons this spirit of deception is so rampant among the brethren. Jesus said, "for MANY shall come..." Not a handful, not a dozen, but "MANY shall come in my name saying I am Christ and shall deceive many." When considering that verse, most in the Church say, *"well, that's cute and all, and that's wonderful to know, and maybe that silliness will happen someday, but how does that apply to our current problems?"*

If right this moment you Googled how many people around the world claim to be the actual literal Jesus Himself, you'd probably be shocked. It's already happening. There are probably more people on planet Earth right now who claim to be the Messiah than at any other time in the history of the world and there are many thousands of people believing their nonsense. There are people in virtually every country of the world, America included, who literally place people upon thrones and carry them around on their shoulders and kiss their feet and proclaim them to be the Son of God. Deceived people who fall into the cultish patterns of the Jim Jones crowd and David Koresh crowd have been around for a very long time. They just happen to get more publicity in the modern era.

There's a man in Brazil right now that has 10,000 members of a church and *they're all women.* They're all women! Makes you wonder where all their men went, right? That's crazy business even before hearing that this cult leader claims to be the Messiah. That's a convenient deception for a pervert, wouldn't you say?

Only One Jesus

Have you figured out why this wave of false Messiah's is suddenly flooding the earth? Because Jesus told us that when the beginning of the end starts ramping up, there's going to be many... there's going to be many... there's going to be MANY that say, "I'm Jesus, I've got the truth." But the one and only Jesus said, "I am the way, I am the truth, and I am the life and no man come to the Father, but by me." (John 4:16)

You don't get to heaven because Jesus is "a" way to heaven, you get to heaven because Jesus is the ONLY way to heaven. For there is no other name given among men, whereby we must be saved! There's only one Jesus, and He's the only way to the Kingdom of God.

Let this mind be in you, which was also in Christ Jesus: Who, being in the form of God, thought it not robbery to be equal with God: But made himself of no reputation, and took upon him the form of a servant, and was made in the likeness of men: And being found in fashion as a man, he humbled himself, and became obedient unto death, even the death of the cross. Wherefore God also hath highly exalted him, and given him a name which is above every name: That at the name of Jesus every knee should bow, of things in heaven, and things in earth, and things under the earth; And that every tongue should confess that Jesus Christ is Lord, to the glory of God the Father.

~ Philippians 2:5-11

So how is it so easy for heretics to fool so many? Because the power of the Word of God in Christendom has become so watered down by church leaders that virtually anything goes these days. If there's a perversion, there's probably a "church" that will embrace it. We all need to grow sick and tired of these mealy-mouthed mamby pamby limp-wristed preachers that won't get up and say, "here's the truth of the Word of God."

There are major evangelical churches, I mean MAJOR evangelical churches, where their pastors go on national TV to say, "You know, there actually may be more than one way to heaven... I don't know... I'm not God, you know, who am I to judge."

Listen, I'm not judging, I'm telling you what the Judge already said. You need Jesus and Jesus alone is the Way. But don't miss the primary point. If you're waiting for a superstar false Jesus to rise to power, that's not what the Bible says.

Wars and Rumors of Wars

And ye shall hear of wars and rumours of wars: see that ye be not troubled: for all these things must come to pass, but the end is not yet. For nation shall rise against nation, and kingdom against kingdom: and there shall be famines, and pestilences, and earthquakes, in divers places.

~ Matthew 24:6-7

"And ye shall hear of wars and rumours of wars..." The talk of wars and rumors of wars of all sorts are rampant no matter where you live. And, of course, everyone in the United States is already talking about the possibility of another civil war. Look, I don't care if it starts in the abortion industry. I don't care if it starts with Black Lives Matter. I don't care if it starts with some wicked secretive group like the KKK. I don't care "where" it starts. You can blame it all on the YouTube Illuminati for all I care. I don't give two flips of a wooden nickel what you call it or where you see it cranking up. I'm here to tell you right now that we are without question living in days when war is about to break out, and these wars will be fought on all types of landscapes—physical, cyber, and spiritual.

We used to think, "*Well you know, that's already been fulfilled because of the long stretch of wars over the past century. We had World War One, then World War Two, then the Korean conflict that kicked off the Cold War, then we had Vietnam, and recently we've had Desert Storm and far too many smaller or secretive wars to count.*"

There's no doubt we've had them all, ladies and gentlemen, and now with the added dimension that is the digital domain of cyberspace, the cryptic meaning of "rumors" has really taken off. Jesus' prophecy of wars and rumors of wars are being fulfilled right now in ways that simply weren't possible before these days, and pockets of people from all around the world have declared war against this nation. Some are literal wars, some are secretive digital wars, some are propaganda wars perpetrated by the mainstream media, and some are merely rumors of wars in each of these domains. But all are mere manifestations of the real war… the war that rages in the spiritual realm against the Church… the war we're all watching unfold in real time. These are those days, and though many were in denial about all this just a few months ago, 2020 has opened a lot of eyes. We're all starting to see it. Even atheists are starting to see it.

The Timeout Generation

If you haven't been paying attention to international events, you might not have noticed that the unprecedented chaos is not a uniquely American phenomenon but is a worldwide trend. Mass protests, violent endless riots, and an overall air of lawlessness and rebellion is exploding everywhere it's allowed. This unrest didn't just bubble up after a singular event.

In Seattle, they finally got rid of CHOP, CHAZ, or whatever you want to call their autonomous zone, where leftist millennials and other groups of disenchanted young people violently chased out the police and other peace-seeking adults. They took over six city blocks in the heart of a downtown community, initially calling it a sovereign nation. How crazy is that? It's never been easier to tell the difference between the timeout generation and the butt whooping generation. Some of these whiny-hiney brats just need a good old-fashioned whooping from grandpa. My granddaddy would have knocked my teeth down my throat (yes, that's hyperbole) if I had treated police officers and respectable adults like that.

Recently in Georgia you might have heard that the Black Panthers mobilized in full military gear… armed with AR-15s, grenades, machine guns… you name it. They gathered in force and plainly stated they wanted to incite a race war. One of the great things about my home church, Global Vision Bible Church, is that we all find the mere thought of a race war as flat out stupidity. It's a repulsive thought to us. We're red and yellow, black and white, tall and short, big and small. We've got black folks, white folks, Latino folks, Asian folks, Italian folks… you name it… all living in unity under one big tent, and NO ONE is a token, so we reject that racism in the face. Every one of our people matter to us.

At Global Vision, we love. We've got crazy people under this tent, and we've got sedate people under this tent, and we have no problem getting along and working through our differences with honesty and peace. But there are groups who feel the only solution to all their problems is to manufacture a race war? Listen, the racial divide in America is not a white situation, and it's not a black situation. We don't have a skin problem; we have a sin problem. Innocent people including women and children are dying in the streets at the hands of evil actors who have no respect for authority… and no fear of the living God. We have to ensure all this lawlessness is corrected.

The Marxist Agenda

Since the riots exploded, every week we've seen police of all colors, both men and women, being ambushed while out on patrol and many have been killed or maimed for life just for trying to serve and protect us... just for trying to do their jobs and provide for their families. Do we see anyone rioting over those outrageous murders week after week? Do we see people stirred up about any of the innocents who are being gunned down in these liberal cities that host these riots and embrace the protestors who embolden and support them?

I don't care how mad people get; we have to speak the truth. BLM is an anti-traditional family, Marxist organization by their own admission, so we will not honor their brand despite the truth of the three very true words they have hijacked. Yes, ALL lives matter, blacks included, but no more than children's lives or women's lives or police lives or pre-born babies' lives. This angry, racist, verbally abusive movement has used intimidation to brainwash good people into believing they aren't good, but are instead racists, and possibly a lower order of human. We've got to reject that ridiculousness before it can do any more damage to our race relations trajectory, which was pointing up in every measurable way before this sudden dramatic crisis.

How could anyone say entering 2020 that a race war was about to break out? There was no such talk. We don't have a race problem. We have a Godlessness problem. We have a lawlessness problem. We have a crime problem, and they believe their Marxist playbook will tear us apart and tear us down. Inciting race wars is their most time-proven tactic. These Marxist groups are mostly comprised of paid actors leading disenfranchised anarchists looking for a place to rage. These trained Marxist-communist agitators, along with their Antifa allies, are funded by elitists who are trying to overthrow our free republic. This isn't just a theory, and it's good to know that most readers are wide awake to the ultimate target of these schemes—the Church.

Not About Race
BLM is entirely anti-Christian in their actions and dogma, and, historically speaking, they've shown very little respect for the life or freedom of anyone they can't exploit… not even black people… not even black children and toddlers… and certainly not black babies in the womb. Yet all these groups are being murdered at unimaginable rates during these days of Democrat-controlled city lawlessness and BLM racism, and none of them seem to care.

These particular black lives don't matter to their mission so they're of no value to them. But they're of value to us, amen? Let's get all that straight about this evil organization. The good people who support them out of ignorance will learn the truth soon enough. As for Antifa, they're just a mob of anarchists and criminals controlled and protected by the same sort of left-wing globalists and their allies in the Democrat party. These are the same forces that have been attempting to overthrow the presidency since the day Donald Trump was elected. Well before then, actually. This is going on right out in the open for all to see, and it's an act of treason or outright war on many levels. These are those days.

Hate Mail from those Who Hate

We had a guy send a message to the church the other day. He said he's been in contact with the head dog at Antifa, and they don't like what we stand for. He lashed out at me for some of my statements in our videos and our podcasts and warned that if I wasn't careful, they would be sending some protesters to our door.

Let me tell you something. Greater is He that is in us than he that is in the world. And if anyone thinks I'm afraid of some kid that smokes meth and hides behind a mask and lives in his momma's basement and needs to grow up and pull up his pants, they're dead wrong. They've picked on the wrong pastor if they plan to bully me or my people.

They've picked on the wrong church if they think my people would be in any way afraid of them. I'm here to tell you, there's a God in heaven and we aren't worried about protesters! We're not bowing down to that mess. At Global Vision Bible Church, the only feet we're kissing are the feet of Jesus.

Another person wrote, *"We're gonna call the Mount Juliet Police Department!"* I told them to go right ahead because the police love us! The local police thank God for our church. We bless them, feed them, honor them, and pray for them without ceasing. Please call the MJPD if you hate us for the way we preach the Gospel.

I was recently involved in a minor vehicle collision (that wasn't my fault, this time!) and an officer showed up and said, "Pastor! How are you doing? Did your daughter tell you that I pulled her over a couple of weeks ago?" I said "No, she quietly left those details out around the dinner table," laughing out loud.

It was a warm conversation full of mutual respect and love. Yet someone wants to call the Mount Juliet Police Department to get them to shut us down or turn against us? Wars and rumors of wars. People are looking for reasons to start fights and social wars and they can't even articulate why they're so mad at us. They're like puppets. In fact, they are puppets; they just don't realize it.

3

Be Not Troubled

The Bible says, "See that ye be not troubled." We all know it, but nearly all of us feel troubled. Isn't that crazy? See that you aren't troubled. Make it so, the Bible says. Yet here we are in the age where many are crying, "Oh my goodness! What are we gonna do?" The answer? Same thing you did yesterday.

Others ask, "What are you going to do when they're burning down the streets of Nashville?" We're still going to gather in the tent, we're still going to preach, we're still going to stand up for righteousness, we're still going to love God, we're still going to love our wives and husbands and kids, we're still going to give selflessly, and we're still going to peacefully and lovingly protest at the local abortion clinic and Planned Parenthoods all over the nation. We're still going to follow the Holy Spirit and keep making a fuss for Jesus, and we're not going to be troubled about all the nonsense going on in the world. Why? Because that nonsense has been going on for a very long time and Jesus said there's going to be even more nonsense every year as His day approaches. The more anarchy we see in the streets, the quicker we get Him back. We really can't lose if we're born again.

Do Not Worry
Don't let it escape you that Jesus directly instructed us not to be troubled when these events are fulfilled. Don't feel threatened. Don't be worried. Don't sit around sucking your thumb and having

a Pauline pity party, crying, "What am I gonna do?" Listen, you've got to live your life. You only get one on this side of glory.

Quit letting the governmental wars and the culture wars burn up your life! Jesus said that all these things MUST COME to pass, and He also said, "But the end is not yet." Jesus was like, just when you're at the climax of the book, guess what? I've still got some chapters for you to wade through... I've still got some stuff you'll have to walk out. The end is not yet, even when we see it coming.

Socio-Political Enemies

As we saw earlier in Matthew 24:7, Jesus said that before the end can come, "nation shall rise against nation." Even as we strengthen our bonds with our true allies, this nation has never faced more socio-political enemies, global and domestic, than we face right now. On the global front, I'm glad our two nations shook hands and sort of made up, but if you think North Korea is our friend you've lost your mind. If you think for one second there is a single Islamic nation on the planet that loves this country, you clearly not paying attention.

I don't tell the members of Global Vision what to do. I do not require masks. Yet every member and visitor could wear a mask and feel just as welcomed as those of us who don't. I certainly don't look down at people who wear a mask. I thank God for people that are health conscious and are aware of their personal vulnerabilities. Maybe you've got a suppressed immune system. If so, it's a great idea to wear a mask or even tune into our service from your car or from your home to help ward off catching a virus.

I don't require masks and I certainly don't besmirch those who wear them. But I will say this to the ladies: It's only a short leap from accepting a regulation that requires you to cover your mouth to accepting Sharia law that requires you to cover your entire head. And if by chance you think I'm just Hocus-Pocus

Kool-Aid peddling, you need to pay attention to what's going on around us.

Israel Always Wins

We have people that openly hate the nation of Israel that are in very high offices of authority in our government. These people have no loyalty to the very nation they are sworn to serve, let alone our most important allies. They just don't like us or the Israeli people. You have to wonder how people who are against our best interests or best allies while praising our real enemies could ever have infiltrated our government.

I'm not saying all of this to throw gasoline on the fire, but to remind you that "nation is going to rise against nation," and sometimes they will rise against us and our allies from within. We're seeing it now. Throughout history, this sort of treasonous division being pushed by evil actors who infiltrate the government is a common precursor to war. But fear not, and don't worry about Israel. Scripture teaches us that in these days, it doesn't matter which nations rise up against Israel. Israel always wins in the end. Isn't that beautiful? Israel always wins. Yet those on the left cry, "My goodness, look at all those beat-down oppressed Palestinians just trying to fight for their homeland." These anti-Israel Islamist terrorists moved into the Holy Land well after it was stolen from the nation of Israel.

All of history records Jerusalem and the Holy Land as the birthplace of the Jewish nation, and the Biblical record plainly records that Jerusalem and the surrounding Holy Land of Judea belongs to Israel. And from a more contemporary perspective, the people of Israel are the oldest people group still on earth who can stake a claim to Israel. This is indisputable.

Feed My Sheep

Nations are going to rise against nations, and kingdom against kingdom, and there shall be famines. It's amazing how many people are starving to death right now in the world. The leading experts are saying that as many as 300 Million could die of starvation worldwide over the coming years due to the Coronavirus shut down. And surely you know there are hungry kids all over America. The most prosperous nation on the earth… the bread basket to the world… and we're letting people starve to death because politicians on the left are unwilling to help us manage this crisis in a way that actually minimizes national and global loss of life through famine and other more prevalent causes of death. They've even invented reasons to shut down and slow down our ability to grow and produce food despite knowing it will leave millions of men, women and children worldwide to die of starvation.

It's amazing how many people our church feeds every single week right here in Wilson County, USA. People are hungry. And yet the Bible tells us there will be famines here and there and everywhere. Even after we get past this COVID overreaction, I believe multiple widespread famines will result from the effects of economic inflation and failed distribution channels. The organizations who work to fight global famines are sounding the alarm as loudly as they can, but the media refuses to give them their audience. That's a new one, but these are those days.

Inflation and the Coin Shortage

Many experts believe inflation will get so bad that basic goods will become unaffordable for most. In time, most people are going to go broke as a joke and begin to feel so small that they could sit on a dime and dangle both legs.

Speaking of dimes, you've probably noticed that almost every convenience store you go to has a sign that says, "We don't have any change because there's a coin shortage." Someone might say, "Oh, brother Locke, you're getting into conspiracy theory, you're getting into some Alex Jones-sized hype." No, I'm telling you what's going on right before your very eyes.

Even if you're not yet a believer, if you'd read the Bible and use your brain, you could see how it all works together as part of a larger plan. Do you know why there's a coin shortage? Because the US mint is going to stop producing coins. Why? So that when you go to the store, if something costs $1.55, the new inflation driven economy will have the stores saying, *"we don't have any coins, so let's just raise it up to $2."*

Very soon, coins are simply not going to be in circulation anymore, because they will have completely stopped producing them. This isn't a conspiracy theory ladies and gentlemen. This is a simple fact.

It's About COMPLIANCE

I'm not a prophet nor a son of a prophet, but if you give it six months, you'll see the Treasury Department start to talk about eliminating paper money as well. You know why? Because they'll eventually devalue our currency so badly that somebody can stand up and say, "our US money is no longer valid, so we'll be transitioning to a universal 'one world' currency."

You see how all this is panning out and lining up for the last days? Again, I'm not making predictions based on my opinion. I'm repeating what many in the government and in high finance are already saying is an inevitability. In fact, it's already happening, and the dark forces are already planning ways to require we take on some sort of chip that can manage all our buying transactions. You might say, *"Well, if I'm still around in those days, I'll tell you one thing, there ain't no way in the world those people are gonna get me to put a mark in my hand... I'm not going to be in compliance."*

Compliance... compliance. If you haven't already figured this out, none of this is about safety. It's about COMPLIANCE. The slow boil has begun, and most are embracing the role of the toad in the pot. This is a good time to jump out.

The Misappropriation of Romans 13

Yes, in Romans 13 the Apostle Paul says we ought to obey the government and the laws of the land. But Romans 13 was also used out of context by Hitler to load 6 million Jews on a bunch of wagons and trains to exterminate them. Romans 13 might contain the most abused Scripture in all the Bible, as kings and religious leaders have used it to abuse the masses since the days of Paul. Yet this passage is in no way a license for the government to override the Word of God. That will never be the case.

Nothing and no one can override the Word of God. We bow to a higher authority than the State House and the White House! Right, wrong, or indifferent, we need to follow the word of God and apply it with our hearts and brains. You might not care what I believe. I may believe one thing about COVID-19—the Coronavirus—or whatever you want to call it, and you may believe something entirely different. That's fine.

Same Old Tricks

I don't deny the reality that people have gotten sick and people have died while having this virus. We reject their reporting of the facts and the statistics. There is so very little honesty in their reporting, and we reject the fear-driven version of reality that the globalists and Marxists and anarchists are using to manipulate the masses into accepting policies that are in direct opposition to the Constitution. This is the sort of tactic Hitler used on the German Church leading up to WWII.

And now we have to navigate through their "more harm than good" shut down plans. When more people are dying of collateral damage caused by the virus shutdown than the actual number of people dying from this virus, the Lord compels us to pause and call them to account. We firmly believe the preponderance of research and front line data prove the reporting agencies are deliberately inflating the numbers for myriad deceptive reasons, most notable among them is their effort to scare people into compliance and keep us in our houses… all while weakening our immune systems and threatening our livelihood through the collapse of our national economy. Evil plans by evil actors. That's what we're standing against.

Hold on to your Hat

Matthew 24:7 in its entirety reads, "For nation shall rise against nation, and kingdom against kingdom: and there shall be famines, and pestilences [diseases and plagues], and earthquakes, in divers places."

We'll continue discussing the ongoing Coronavirus pestilence in a bit, but did you know that statistically there are more earthquakes occurring around the world right now than at any time in recorded human history? Earthquakes occur all over the planet, even under the sea, and the whole earth is groaning. Personally, I'm still waiting for that big one to happen. You know, the one with the dotted line along the eastern California border. Maybe that whole liberal mess can just break off and sail out in the ocean to form its own socialist island state.

Revelation 6:14 says the earthquakes are going to be so big that every mountain is going to shake out of its place and the land masses are going to be removed from their foundation. Yes, even scientists are telling us the big one is coming, and earthquakes and other major natural disasters beyond anything we've ever seen have already begun. And while it's easy to remain calm and even lighthearted when discussing these events before they happen, when this sort of global cataclysm finally occurs, it will surely end civilization as we know it.

On top of all that, just when I thought 2020 was going to start easing up to give us a bit of a break, Kanye West said he was running for president. My goodness. I tell you what, if it wasn't for Trump, I'd vote for him. I like that guy! He's pushing back against the darkness as best he can, and we can only encourage folks who see what is going on in the spiritual realm. We know Jesus warned us that things are going to get desperate during these harrowing days but brace yourself for what He says next.

All these are the beginning of sorrows.   ~ *Matthew 24:8*

Holy smokes. The reason Jesus said that "these are the beginning of sorrows" is because this is truly just the beginning. The apocalyptic year of 2020 is just the beginning? That's what He said, so we really haven't seen anything yet.

It's Going to Get Worse

Now, let me share with you as your friend just for a minute. I promise I'm not going to be *spooktacular*, and I'm not going to say crazier stuff than I've already said. My wife can attest to this. We were driving up the road the other day returning home from preaching in Florida when I said, "Honey, let me tell you what I am anxious about." Now, I know I'm to be anxious for nothing, but please don't preach at me... I know.

Let me be transparent for a minute. I feel the Lord compelling me to tell you what can make me anxious in my spirit from time to time. It's been four or five months of hell for many in this nation. But I know—I think we all know—that we have just now scratched the sticker on the chaos. I'm going to tell you what I believe is about to happen just so you know where I am spiritually when it happens.

In October we're going to see the biggest "media peak" in Coronavirus cases that we've yet to see, and you'll be hearing about fear-inducing spikes in the most curious places. These deceptions are an example of "the beginning of sorrows." But it won't all be propaganda. Things are going to get so bad that the mobs are going to start burning down large buildings and entire neighborhoods. And if it continues to go unchecked, Inflation is going to rise so high that even a loaf of bread will be hard to find—If you can afford it.

Darker Days to Come

The chaos and craziness are going to get so ramped up that it's going to change the atmosphere and the landscape of the American Church forever. We can see how it has already been changed over just a few months of 2020. I am convinced that after the November 3rd election the culture in America as we know it will begin to disappear. It just will. The Lord may choose to tarry to give us more time, but Jesus warns us not to ever live as if He will delay His return. Through it all, we'll make progress where we move in His authority, but things are going to get far worse, and I'm commanded to alert you to these facts (Matthew 24:45-51).

No matter who wins the election, these riots are not going away. They may ebb and flow a bit while they prepare for the next wave, but the fact is they're about to intensify until domestic terrorism eventually takes over as their primary form of warfare. It's a familiar pattern. We see them tearing down statues, we hear the defamation of our nation and the desecration of our history, and we see them trying to erase the memory of our founders. And though it has eased up a bit as the election approaches, it's still just now beginning. It is going to get darker, it is going to get more insidious, it is going to grow more widespread, and the leaders of the rebellions are going to become far more brazen and terribly violent.

Now that they've shown their hand, they simply can't put this chaos back in the box. With every violent advance, the anarchists are going to be treated as heroes by the mainstream media, and those of us that say anything against them are going to be treated as their enemies and targets of their rage. No matter what happens in this election, all of this destruction will eventually come to pass. But don't be deceived, it is all going to happen sooner than we want. It's not a matter of *if*, but *when,* and it could be any day now (Matthew 24:44).

4

They Shall Deliver You Up

*Then shall they deliver you up to be afflicted, and shall kill you:
and ye shall be hated of all nations for my name's sake.*

~ Matthew 24:9

Let's think about this for a minute. This is one of the passages that
I used to have a very difficult time believing as a pastor. People are
going to "deliver us up," or turn us over to our persecutors? Yes.
Normal people we know, even some we love, will literally turn on
us. The Bible says that in these days Brother will be against
brother and a father will be against his son, and so on… in the
darkest ways imaginable (Matthew 10:21).

Before 2020, when I would read Jesus' end times
prophecies I would always be like, "Whoa, whoa, wait a minute.
Lord, You just said that? You Lord Jesus… and it's recorded in red
letters in the Word of God? Lord, You just said that in the last days
that these people will turn us over to authorities knowing they will
afflict us and perhaps even kill us. How could this be?"

When I would read that in the past I used to think, "who
could ever be that cold, that destructive, that divisive, that brazen?"
And what could ever drive people we know in our communities—
even those we love—to betray us in the public forum?" I couldn't
imagine it. Then COVID-19 happened.

The COVID-19 Affect

Suddenly a mysterious virus that originated in the largest communist nation in the world, shrouded in deception and secrecy, has become the most polarizing, most divisive issue of our generation. You wouldn't believe how many times people have called the police asking that we get arrested for gathering as a church, or how many folks have gone out of their way to take pictures of our church gatherings because we don't require masks.

They actually want us to be persecuted for exercising our 1st Amendment rights—rights they believe should be suspended—just because they're consumed with unfounded fear. You wouldn't believe my inbox on Twitter. What I see most mornings just after waking up would shock you. I wouldn't even read some of these messages in mixed company. I don't know if I'd read many even amongst all men. Truly perverse and demonic threats.

Some people ask why we have a big safety team and a mobile security force. They think we're being paranoid. But when I show them a couple of the texts that contain detailed death-threats they change their tune quick. We trust the Lord, and part of that trust involves ensuring our people are always safe, just as Jesus taught. If people want to sit in their cars while joining a service, bless God, let them do it. If some want to wear a mask, we welcome them too, but we're never going to require masks.

No Longer a Mystery

A few days ago, I woke up to one of the most red-hot, blisteringly crazy news media articles against me that I've ever seen, and others posting it to Twitter were adding the hashtag "Jim Jones Jr." simply because of my stance on masks. I don't believe we should force an entire congregation into compliance with mandates from a tyrannical lawless government that's buck wild and out of control.

Again, I no longer wonder how and why people are going to start turning each other in to be persecuted. Do you know how many people walk around looking for people to turn in these days?

It's almost like a hunting game to them, and we're their prey. People go to Walmart and they look for folks that aren't wearing a mask. I can hear it now, "911, what's your emergency?"

Caller: "There's somebody in the candy aisle and they ain't got a mask on!" Speed ahead a few months and tell me you don't believe they're eventually going to turn people in when they refuse to take the mark or the chip or whatever it ends up being. Give it a test. Tell people that you and your family aren't going to take the vaccination and see what happens. First, they'll look at you like a Billy goat eating briars. Then many will start wondering how the government will make sure you comply... "for our safety," and they'll assist however they can... "for our safety."

When it's all said and done, I'm going to have to stand before God and answer for how I led our church in Mount Juliet and online, so we're not going to lay down. We're not going to roll over. We're going to stand up. We're going to push back ladies and gentlemen, because we are living in the days when Jesus is coming again sooner than we think. I'm not going to be a coward, and I'm not going to teach you to be a coward. Instead, we're going to be salt and light to a world that desperately needs truth and hope.

Hated by Haters

As we read earlier in Matthew, Jesus told us that we would be hated by all nations for His namesake. God's people will be truly hated. This sort of hate might not have seemed possible just a year ago, but in 2020 they've made us the enemy. They don't even honor Dr. Martin Luther King, Jr. anymore, because he was a Christian who protested the way the Apostles would have protested... defiantly but peacefully, standing firm on the truth but ready to suffer persecution if necessary. He wasn't an anarchist who terrorized communities the way Marxists have always done it. Marxist socialist communists—whatever you want to call them— hate Christianity more than anything. These domestic Marxists already said *"cancel Christianity, Christianity is the problem, it's the worst religion in the world, they're causing all the problems, they've always caused the problems, Christians are killing people... etc., etc."*

We have folks right now, right this second, that believe I'm somehow killing their grandparents in Nashville, Tennessee just because I'm meeting in a tent with large groups of people. Over and over I read this sort of illogical, unscientific attack on my freedoms. I've seen hundreds of variations, but they're all screaming, "You murderous thing you!" If I continue obeying and defending the law of God and the law of the land by rejecting these illegal mandates, I'll probably be getting this sort of treatment for the rest of my life.

Just this morning someone sent me a message that said, *"I hope you die in a horrible car accident, and if you don't, I hope you kill yourself and rid your church of the vermin that you are."*

Nice people. Now look, I'm no better than anybody else. But I know some folks that would drop the microphone and walk away from the place the Lord has me, and most would just change the subject and get back in step with the masses. It's no fun being hated this way, and I'm going to be honest with you. Someone is going to have to put a leash on me if this keeps up. If the way I preach and teach the word of God right now makes you nervous, wait until November gets here. I'm going to continue standing firm in the Lord and stay the course no matter what happens. A dark violent spirit has been loosed on this land, and that's a genie you can't just put back in the bottle. We need to be ready.

Calling it as I See it

You can trust I'm never going to cow down to this mess, and I pray you'll join me. I'm going to keep on speaking out on everything the Lord whispers in my ear, and every single word of God wherever it is needed. I recently got a stronger battery pack that made my bullhorn twice as loud, and I'm ready to use it.

As I pause to consider whether or not you are in agreement at this point, I realize a few of you will be thinking *"holy macaroli I don't know if I can finish reading this book."* That's cool, that's all right. You can always find some cotton candy skittles and unicorns book by a preacher who just tells you what you want to hear and strokes your ego and talks about how great you are, and reminds you that every day is a Friday, and says "you'll never have any problems if you serve God." That's heresy right there. According to Jesus, if you really serve God it might not turn out so hot for you in these last days. It's time to stand up. It's time to get ready.

Taking Offense

And then shall many be offended, and shall betray one another, and shall hate one another.

~ Matthew 24:10

Jesus then tells us that in the last days, "many shall be offended." Isn't that one of the key identifying factors of the generation we're living in? People can suddenly claim to be offended by anything at any time, even if it's your free speech opinion spoken in a constructive way. People are offended by statues of people that liberated us. They're even offended by people and institutions that have helped our nation survive and thrive. Why? Because these people are ignorant to history, and they prefer to remain ignorant. Many of these folks only know what they learn on Twitter and they don't want to discuss the truth when it goes against their groupthink. Their world view erases any reason to discuss ours. We just have to shut our mouths and go away. "Many shall be offended."

When God Offended Me

You know how I got saved? I got offended. God offended me with my sin. He offended me while I was in rebellion. He offended me

41

with my depravity. He offended me with my disobedience, and that's when I got born again 28 years ago. People get offended by everything these days, but instead of growing, they flip out and act out. I'm thinking about starting a new campaign, and I'll call it *I'm offended that you're so offended.*

Let me be direct. It's not like you can spread offense like a disease, right? Okay, so your feelings are hurt. Are you going to die from it or spread it to others? Does it hurt so badly that you need to scream? It's not like you stubbed a tender toe. That would be an offense worthy of screaming. But simply reading something that hurts your cotton candy feelings, ladies and gentlemen, if that stuff upsets you, you clearly needed to feel it.

We all need to get over ourselves in this world. Back in the day we all agreed on that. But suddenly in this generation, if you're not politically correct, if you're not PC, if you're not "woke," they believe in something called the cancel culture. "If you offend us, we will cancel you." They're trying to cancel all the late-night talking heads, they're trying to cancel NASCAR, and they're trying to cancel all the sports that don't bow to them. They're trying to cancel outspoken singers and actors and athletes who don't agree with them.

Worst of all they're trying to cancel anyone that says anything that promotes Jesus, or President Trump, or conservative principles in general. This is the cancel culture, invented by people who get offended by everything and readily get mad about nonsense just because they can. It's a crazy sort of Marxist bullying tyranny, but somehow, they've been getting away with it.

Many False Prophets
And many false prophets shall rise, and shall deceive many.

~ Matthew 24:11

Let me promise you something. I will never be one of those false prophets. This is why I only teach the Bible. I have my theories and I always have a word of encouragement for the people, but if it's not in the Bible, you won't hear me getting fired up about it. I will never risk becoming one of those individuals that lead people astray with predictions that aren't validated in the Bible.

I'm not saying that everything I say is perfectly framed or that my opinions and theories are always right. I've learned well that neither is true. What I'm saying is that everything I read from the Bible is absolutely correct. I might have some strong personal opinions and you can trust I'll always let you know when it's theology or Locke-ology, because there is a difference. You don't have to agree with my opinions, but you're foolish if you don't agree with the Bible. My confidence in what I know to be true is based entirely on my absolute faith in the inerrant word of God.

Wolves in Sheep's Clothing
In Matthew Chapter 7 Jesus said, in effect, that in the day of His return many shall say unto Him, Lord, Lord, did we not cast out devils, did we not write books, did we not do great things, did we not feed the homeless, did we not prophesy and preach and pray in your name? And then Jesus will say to them, "*I never knew you, depart from me you workers of iniquity, and enter the everlasting fire prepared for the devil and his angels.*"

As always, it's important to know the context of such a loaded passage. In Matthew 7:15, Jesus said, "*Beware of false prophets, which come to you in sheep's clothing, but inwardly they are ravening wolves.*"

Many of the people who fall for the lies of false prophets will go to hell. Sad but true, and my job is to help steer people clear of that dread destination.

Waxing Cold

And because iniquity shall abound, the love of many shall wax cold.

~ *Matthew 25:12*

Jesus is telling us that betrayals and sin will become so common that they happen in the shameless broad daylight. The persecution of the Church is only going to get worse, and it will eventually become overwhelming. Jesus isn't talking about lost people here, he's talking about believers. Because iniquity shall abound, because perversity will be so accepted, because it will be so readily available, because we will begin to look like the enemy when we stand against it or even when we preach and pray and prophesy against it.

Believers will be framed by the media and the masses as the bad guys, and the bold voices for Christ will become public enemy number one. Sin will become so tolerated and accepted in the church that the love of many "shall wax cold." Do you know what the phrase "wax cold" means? It means that over time a believer who was once hot with passion for the Lord will become as one repeatedly dipped in a sealing wax that hardens, and as the hardening wax takes hold, the passion lessens, and lessens, and lessens—until it is cold as ice—and the wax not only chokes out your fire but it also blinds and deafens you to the truth.

If you wax cold you will care less about the gathering of the family of God. You'll care less about the truth of God's word. You'll care less about solid preaching. And pretty soon you'll get to a place where you'll even doubt the validity and the authority and the assurance of your own salvation because you will grow cold in your faith. You will be afraid to stand up and afraid to be seen as one who is passionately on fire for Jesus, because fear of what the offenders say about you shuts your mouth and further cements the wax.

44

Many will be offended and because of that iniquity shall abound. They are already marching in our streets, and I'm not talking about BLM in this case, but these people that say, *"we have a right to indoctrinate your children with sexual perversion if we so jolly well please… we're going to have more and more drag queen story hours at the local tax-paid-for libraries where full grown balding men dress up like sexualized women with short skirts and sit on a stool while telling kids that it's okay to pick whatever bathroom or whatever locker room they want to, because gender no longer matters to us."*

These people believe they have the right to tell our children that boys aren't always boys and girls aren't always girls, and that people like me who agree with science and the Bible are transphobic, homophobic, racist, sexist bigots. And because "iniquity shall abound" the Church will be in retreat, crying, *"oh my goodness, preacher, don't grab a microphone and say anything about that… don't let people know that the rainbow is a sign of faithfulness created by God, and not a symbol of perversion created by the LGBTQ crowd."* I'm not retreating with them, and I hope you'll stand with me.

Concerning Our Children
The rainbow belongs to God ladies and gentlemen, and it has always been a holy symbol, but when iniquity abounds and the love of believers waxes cold, look how easily we can surrender a symbol once so precious, especially in children's ministries. When they can so easily pervert the beauty of a rainbow or teach our children to believe there are more than two sexes or that it's hateful to call their behavior sinful and receive zero push-back from the Church for trying to pervert our children's minds, you have to start asking what's next? What other part of our children's minds are we going to let them control? Most people swallowed this lock down and agreed to submit way too quickly.

We're getting too comfortable with letting the world dictate our way of life and decide what we teach our children about good and evil, right and wrong. We're living in days where we've given an entire month to celebrate anti-science, anti-Christian perversion in this nation. If we ever campaigned to set aside a month to celebrate Judeo-Christian morality the way they do their favorite new deviation, they would probably burn our church down. That might have seemed like impossible hyperbole just a few months ago, but now we're all holding our breath. If we don't regain control of our rights, mass church burnings could soon be coming to a neighborhood near you. Thus the silence among most pastors… the waxing has begun.

I Will Not Be Moved

As I write all this, I'm set ablaze with conviction! Christians are laying down on the job, too terrified to speak their minds. I've heard many explain, "Well, if I say anything, I might lose my job." Maybe you don't need that particular job! I'm done with this nonsense, and I'm failing you miserably if I don't spark a sense of urgency in you during this dark season. I'm never backing down, and I'll never bow in trembling to anyone but the Lord. I hope you'll join me. I'm going to love people till the moment I die. I'll reach them, support them, pray over them, pray for them, pray with them, and even heal them if called to in Jesus' name.

If you think for one minute I'm going to compromise my calling or my values and capitulate to this culture through fear or manipulation or threats against my life, I. WILL. NOT. BE. MOVED!!! I pray this is true of you. I'm grateful for a church that supports me, but I'd speak out this way even if they threw tomatoes at me. I'd preach this way if they threw stones at me. It has already begun. I'm not in this to win friends and influence people. I'm in this to influence and impact people for the Kingdom of God through Christ Jesus.

The Reward for Standing Firm

In Matthew 24:13 Jesus said, "But he that shall endure unto the end, the same shall be saved." Be assured that it's not the endurance to stand firm to the end that saves you. This endurance is the product and evidence of a life that has already been saved through Jesus. People who have truly given their lives to Christ and are truly saved and born again are the only ones who will truly endure, truly stand firm, unto the end. God's true people are going to stay the course no matter what comes against us. God's people are going to stand firm through every persecution. God's people are going to continue being salt and light and preach the Gospel unto the end, even unto death. It's the mark of the saved. For that, we are not to be consumed with an effort to anticipate the day the end will come.

Jesus tells us that no one will know the day or hour the end will come, not even the angels, but only God, so we need to stay about His business (Matthew 24:36). Knowing that the end has not yet come, and can be delayed, we should be emboldened by the fact we still have life to live and persecution to stand against, just as Jesus told us.

5

That Different Kind of Dream

One of the reasons I felt compelled to explore this passage despite its heaviness is because of an unforgettable dream I had just a few weeks ago. On that particular night I had a hard time sleeping for a number of reasons, and when I finally fell asleep, I was suddenly jolted up out of bed by the Lord. It was 1:24 AM, and I quickly grabbed my phone to write it down in my notes.

As a caveat, let me say what I'm not saying. I do not believe for one second in extra-Biblical revelation, okay? If it can't be verified by the Bible or harmonize seamlessly with the promises of God found in the Bible, I don't deal with it. So whatever you believe God tells you in dreams or visions, it can't contradict the Bible… or it's not from God.

I agree that God still speaks through dreams and visions and the discernment of the Holy Spirit who dwells within us once we're born again. Don't doubt that. But these "words" must always be in line with Biblical prophecy and teaching, amen?

Jesus teaches us that we may not know the exact time of a particular event, but we can definitely discern the seasons, and we're living in a season today that should have us all soberly expectant. When people started prophesying over me and telling me things they believed came from the Lord, I've typically resisted. It's important that you know I've been the most non-charismatic person that you've probably ever met. I grew up Baptist… a fundamentalist Baptist at that. Throughout my seminary training and many years thereafter it was ingrained in me to resist any form of the prophetic, and I have had to unlearn a lot of stuff when God started showing up doing things that didn't fit my fundamentalist theological training. But here we are, and the Holy Spirit is compelling me to share something with you.

Wake Up Call

I've only had a couple of experiences in my life where God revealed something to me in my sleep. Each time I woke up and I knew, oh my goodness, that was the real deal, Lucile. It didn't contradict the Bible, and when it dealt with something that had yet to happen that eventually happened, it always grew my faith. A lot of you can relate. When a rare dream of future events harmonizes with the Bible and eventually comes to pass, it's right to search the word to gain understanding and avoid over-spiritualizing the experience. God primarily speaks to me through the Bible, and God also speaks to me through people. I'm not one of these folks who believe I have the gift of God speaking frequently to me through dreams and visions. Some of you have that gift, and I thank God for it as long as it is Biblical and as long as it's not silly. If it doesn't contradict the Book, I'm all for it.

When I had that crazy dream that woke me up at 1:24, I knew it wasn't from Greg, and it wasn't from bad pizza. It was from God, and for once, I somehow knew He wanted me to share it despite the fact that "I'm not that kind of pastor." I'm just being transparent, so don't let my personal experience with dreams and visions get in the way of the reason the Lord gave me this particular dream… because I believe it was not just for me, but for all of us. I have friends who watch me online that will give me more grief and criticism for this unexpected realization in my ministry than anything else I've ever shared. But I'm telling you… I was in the middle of a very real experience and God just woke me up and said, "write it down… write it down now… or you're going to forget to write it down." And so I did, at 1:24 in the morning. I had never done this before. I've preached for 28 years and never, not once, have I told people in a public forum something that God told me or showed me in a dream. I hope it speaks to you.

This Is What I Saw

In the dream I was surrounded by people from my church, Global Vision, but we weren't in the building that we currently call home. Though I see it clearly, I don't recognize the building, but that seems inconsequential. Here's what I know is of consequence in this dream.

Government agencies had cut off the power to our lights and had blocked our parking lot, but members and visitors kept trying to get in. I could recognize many of the people, but I didn't know exactly who they were. I just knew they were our peeps. And this went on for about an hour, then two hours, then a few more hours went by. Despite the lack of lights, no one would leave. All the while I kept apologizing, "They'll get the lights back on soon folks, they'll turn the lights back on... so don't leave, please don't leave!" I just kept telling them we've got to preach, and we've got to pray, and we've got to worship the Lord. I just kept pleading, "Don't leave!" But the active effort to shut us down just kept on increasing. They were making every effort to shut us down, and I kept pleading.

Finally, something just happened. I don't know how, but the lights suddenly came back on. Everybody started rejoicing… just clapping and shouting praise to the Lord. It's still as vivid in my memory as it could possibly be. My wife Tai and I walked up the aisle and I remember getting up on the platform, still noticing that it was a very different building. It was sort of small, but long, and now it was all lit up.

As I approached the pulpit, I noticed I was wearing a suit and tie. You'd think that would have woken me up because I can hardly remember the last time I got dressed up to preach at my home church. But I remember it was at that point that I started weeping, and I said to all in the church, "I'm sorry, I don't have any control over the powers that be, and they're trying to cut off our lights and they're trying to shut us down and they're trying to keep us from worshiping and I don't know what's going on."

While I was speaking—I'm telling the God's honest truth—while I was apologizing, I noticed a man who was one of our people. I don't know which of our men it was, but in the dream, I knew him well. He was sitting about three rows away from me. And suddenly, a blue flame flickered up over his head. Pow... it just flickered up, and I was so stunned that I stopped talking. And then, all of a sudden, pow, pow, pow...blue flames started flickering up all through the crowd, one after another. And suddenly, I started crying big time, and was shouting at the top of my lungs and praising God with every fiber of me, and my wife was sitting like two feet from me to my right, and she had this look on her face that was like, "What on earth is happening here?"

Write It Down

And about that time as I continued watching this chain reaction spreading through the church…. POW! I could sense that Tai could also see what I was seeing in the dream. And when I whipped around to look at her again... POW! Her blue flame was so close to me I could have reached out and touched it. And I'm telling you, I started praying with all my heart in the midst of that dream. I mean just screaming out to God, crying, with blue flames hovering overhead all across the building.

Right in the middle of this beautifully intense prayer I suddenly woke up. I went from my deepest state of sleep and I just jolted upright in my bed. It was like God snapped his fingers in my ear and whispered, "Write it down!" I'll admit right now that I had a hard time processing all of that experience, because it was far more than a normal dream. I do know that a blue flame is the hottest flame. I do know that in the second chapter of Acts when the Holy Spirit poured out upon the believers during Pentecost, there were cloven tongues of fire that came upon each of the 120 disciples who were present, and each was filled to the full with the Holy Ghost. Each disciple then began to pour out onto the busy streets of Jerusalem to speak the word of GOD with BOLDNESS.

Some even spoke in foreign languages they didn't previously know so that all the pilgrims from around the world who were in the streets celebrating the festival could understand the Gospel and believe in Jesus. This historic event obviously turned the world upside down. That's what I DO know, and that's where my dream clearly harmonizes with the Bible.

I've got to tell you, many people are going to be upset when they read this, but nothing I've written or will write about this dream will ever contradict the Bible. I believe with all my heart, in the core of my being, that the following is what the Lord is telling me through this dream.

I'm confident that persecution against the Church is exactly what is going to trigger the outpouring of the Holy Spirit fire... Pow. Pow. Pow. POW! I also believe this outpouring is going to spark the hottest revival fire that we've ever experienced. The fact that my dream wasn't filled with small orange and red flickering flames, but super-hot blue flames speaks directly to that interpretation. Not only is this fiery revival going to break out during times of intense "shut down" persecution, but these acts of persecution are exactly what's going to bring the Holy fire. Additionally, during the dream I found it interesting that the first flicker... POW... came upon a man.

Send the Fire!

My wife and all who truly know me will attest that I'm no misogynist sexist, so this has nothing to do with a special honor bestowed upon men—on the contrary. Through this man in the dream, the Lord revealed to me what needs to happen before the revival fire is going to fall on local churches like ours at Global Vision, and not a day before. When the men truly get right with God... when the men get openly fired up for Jesus Christ and truly fall in love with Him, and when the men selflessly fall in love with their families and lay their lives down for them…. then and only then will men begin to fall on their faces and repent of their sins and wicked ways and cry out to God to send the fire! Send the fire! SEND THE FIRE! That's when it's going to happen—when the men get right with God!

Thank God for the women who keep the Church alive! Thank God for these spirit-filled ladies, but we need the men to get right with God once and for all! We need the men to stand up and lead in areas that they've abdicated or simply ignored. I don't know all that God is doing to prepare us, but I'll tell you this, when they finally cut off the lights, when they say all manner of evil against us for His name's sake, when they begin to slander Jesus in ways that are too hard to bear, and when they start to barricade the roads to churches and padlocking church doors to keep us from gathering, let me tell you the only thing I'm going to be looking for POW! POW! POW!

Closing Prayer

Will you pray with me as we close? Lord, we need revival. Lord, sometimes we say we need an old-fashioned revival, but we know now that we actually need a NEW-fashioned revival... we need what we've never seen before. We're not asking to see something we might have read in a book somewhere. We need to see something of a Biblical God-sized proportion. Send your Holy Spirit flame, oh God. Bless every person that is reading this Lord, but I feel like You want us to specifically ask you to set the men on fire with your Spirit. God, I pray that you use all we're watching come to pass to wake up the Church according to your Word in this season. There's no way we can deny the reality of everything that is unfolding before our very eyes. It's just so real, so raw. Lord we can see it, sense it, smell it, touch it, taste it. It's everywhere. Your Word is being fulfilled, and you said to work while it's yet day because the night comes when no man can work. Wake up the workers Lord! I know some think we're crazy. I know people think I can be arrogantly jerkish at times. So I pray, Holy Spirit, that you'll help me to find your line between boldness and belligerence. Lord, I don't want to be a jerk, and I don't want any men to act out like jerks. But I don't want men to become cowards either. I can handle being slandered by the world, but I never want to be called a coward by You, oh God. So Father, choose us to sound Your battle cry. I believe you're thinning out the ranks in the global church, but you're also raising up an army. And I pray You do it quickly, in the mighty name of Jesus, amen.

Part II: Persecution

Blessed are they which are persecuted for righteousness' sake: for theirs is the Kingdom of heaven. Blessed are ye, when men shall revile you, and persecute you, and shall say all manner of evil against you falsely, for my sake. Rejoice, and be exceeding glad: for great is your reward in heaven: for so persecuted they the prophets which were before you. Ye are the salt of the earth: but if the salt have lost his savour, wherewith shall it be salted? it is thenceforth good for nothing, but to be cast out, and to be trodden under foot of men. Ye are the light of the world. A city that is set on an hill cannot be hid. Neither do men light a candle, and put it under a bushel, but on a candlestick; and it giveth light unto all that are in the house. Let your light so shine before men, that they may see your good works, and glorify your Father which is in heaven. ~Jesus

Matthew 5:10-16

6

COVID-19 and the Local Church

I used to spend a lot of time wondering if I would ever actually see true Bible prophecy being fulfilled before my very eyes. I have always struggled to see how it could ever be possible for our government to convince the Church that it was non-essential and needed to follow mandates and regulations that would "shut it up" and render it irrelevant. The scenario always seemed like it would have to take place far off in the future. I suppose we've all exposed ourselves to so many apocalyptic sci-fi movies that we just assumed it would one day happen, but certainly not in our lifetime... not while the Church still held so much influence in this nation and around the world. 2020 has changed all of that.

I am convinced that we have taken a 50-year prophetic leap in this single year alone. Don't get me wrong, the Lord has done some unbelievable things on our behalf. But the Left has been able to dig in, stand up, and push the church of the Living God into a corner of silence. Our silence has now become our surrender. Let me say that again Church. Our silence has become our surrender.

We have so compromised our core values and have so watered down our message that no one takes us seriously anymore. All it took was a media-infused virus to show the true colors of the cowardly pastors in the fear-filled churches all across this great nation. We have literally laid down, rolled over, and given them the authority to stop us from preaching the most powerful message on the planet. What is wrong with us? How in the world did the most powerful movement God ever created become so spineless, so weak, so powerless?

Prayer

In Part 2 I want to give you the Biblical basis and primary strategies for being the Church in these days of persecution. First, please join me in this prayer. Father, no one is reading this book by accident. Not a man, not a woman, not a boy, not a girl. We've all come into the Kingdom for such a time as this, and how blessed we are to be alive in this generation. I pray that you would use this section concerning persecution to encourage our hearts and to free us from our fears. Lord, whether the reader is a new believer in desperate need of a touch from you today, or a longtime Christian in need of revival to shake them from their lukewarm faith, or a lifelong fence straddler looking for the truth, Lord, I pray right now that a spirit of awakening would fall on all of us and fill our hearts with your presence. Lord, use your word to do what Greg Locke cannot do, and give us a boldness that can only come from you. We thank you for all you're preparing to do in us and in the Church and in all the world, in the magnificent mighty name of Jesus, our Savior. Amen.

Preaching to a Tone-Deaf Choir

I recently sat in my car in the parking lot of a coffee shop crying out to the Lord in utter disbelief of what is happening all around us. It doesn't even seem like the Church is paying attention these days. Do you not realize that God has already predicted all of this? Has it not occurred to us that we are the very picture of the Laodicean church as described in the Book of Revelation? The longer I sat there and prayed, the more spiritually frustrated I became. So I picked up my phone, shot a quick video on the fly, and within 2 days millions of people had seen it. Our church office began receiving messages from pastors all over the county demanding an apology. The following is the exact transcript from the video.

Video Message to COVID Compliant Pastors

You know, there is so much going on in our nation right now it's hard to keep up with. But one of the things that I'm just uber-frustrated and discouraged about is the reaction that churches are having to the government-mandated shutdowns. *"Well, you know that Romans Chapter 13 says that we ought to obey the government."* Romans Chapter 13 used out of context is how Hitler loaded six million Jews in boxcars and tried to exterminate an entire ethnicity.

Look, I recognize that it's not about a building. It's not about a location. The power is not in an auditorium. The power is in the gathering ladies and gentlemen. And we have zapped the power because we have done away with the gathering. It's not where you worship. It's not how you worship. It's WHO you worship. And "the power"... Hebrews says, Romans says, Acts says, the Gospels teach... "the power" is in the gathering of God's people together.

And now we're not gathering. California is a hotbed for this nonsense and now Texas shockingly is following suit. Look, I pastor in Nashville. We never closed one time. I'm not bragging, I'm just stating the facts. We didn't close one time. And come hell or high water, Jesus is the only thing that will snatch us out of here to make us close our church. We're not closing the doors of our church for a pandemic. Okay? We're not going to make people "social distance." We're not going to have half-size auditoriums and make people wear masks.

This isn't Haiti, okay? This isn't some sort of Iraq. This is the United States of America. We're not meeting in some third world country. We're not under communism. This isn't Venezuela. This is the United States of America. And now Governor Newsome says, *"Well, you know churches can't sing,"* and *"we don't want you to gather,"* and *"it's dangerous."* Let me tell you what's dangerous. It's dangerous for these mamby pamby pastors to use out-of-context Bible verses to try to tell their people, *"it's okay, let's just worship online! It's okay, just stay home! It's only going to be for a couple of weeks! Hey! Fifteen days to slow the spread!"* That was MONTHS ago ladies and gentlemen and we're still trying to "slow the spread" over something that's NOT spreading. AT ALL. The numbers are going up and the death rate is going DOWN. I'm telling you we've been lied to, we've been duped, we've been deceived. OPEN the churches!

Be courageous Pastor! LEAD through some of this nonsense. Some of you people ought to stand up TO your pastor and say, *"Pastor...open the doors of the church! Quit pandering to the left!"* This is getting so nonsensical. I'm telling you; we are DESTROYING the local church of the Lord Jesus Christ in the United States because we're trying to placate to a culture that hates God in the first place.

Jesus said the gates of hell shall not prevail against His church (Matthew 16:18). And if you think the government is going to prevail, you think COVID, some kind of pandemic is going to prevail, you think the left is going to prevail? No ladies and gentlemen. We are being destroyed not from the outside in, we're being destroyed from the inside out. We have got to push back against this nonsense. OPEN your churches! This is ridiculous.

There was a time when it all started, I thought, "well, I'm not gonna shame anybody for not [opening]..." I've CHANGED my shame-game a thousand percent. I've changed my shame-game. You know why? Because now you OUGHT to be shamed. Because you ought to have your church open. And you ought to let people worship and hear preaching and pray and fast and give and show up for the fellowship of believers because again, the location isn't the power, the gathering... the gathering... THE GATHERING... is the POWER of God ladies and gentlemen, and we have got to get back to preaching the Gospel of Jesus Christ.

ENOUGH with all this padlocking the church doors... *"let's just go online."* NO. Enough, enough. I don't care if you're a mega-church. I don't care if you're a church that has five people. Open the door! We have closed the hope centers of the United States. We need hope now more than ever. We need Jesus more than ever. We need preaching more than ever. We need the Bible and the authority of the Holy Spirit more than ever. We need to see God do something more than ever. And what are we doing? We're sitting around in our pajamas on our couches sipping lattes with not enough power to blow the fuzz off a small peanut. Open up your churches!

I don't care how mad you get. I don't care how upset. You can unfollow me and you can report me. People can get mad and say whatever they want to. I don't live under communism. I live under the Constitution of this great nation, which is still great and still free. And most of all, I live under the authority and the influence of a book that we call the Bible. So I'm telling you churches, and I'm telling you pastors, get a backbone, stand up, PUSH BACK against this garbage, OPEN UP THE CHURCHES. There is absolutely zero excuse for any church in America being closed right now over this COVID nonsense.

OPEN THE CHURCHES, and let's watch revival fire fall!

No Apologies This Time

I had no idea that this four-minute video would cause such a stir. Apparently, it struck a massive nerve in the Body of Christ. Apologize? What in the world would I apologize for? As I write this, I am more convinced than ever that the Church in America is a compromised mess.

Sitting on my desk is a heartbreaking letter from a fellow Pastor. He was commending me for my boldness and at the same time lamenting that if he took the same stand, he would be asked to step down from the church he has pastored for 16 years. What!?!

That doesn't sound like the stance of a local New Testament church. It's utter nonsense that flies in the face of all the Lord instructs pastors—especially in seasons of great persecution like this. That sounds more like a coffee drinking social club trying to stay in business by pandering to the fear mongers who dictate their actions... or lack thereof. We have major "Evangelical" leaders that have already postponed in-house worship services until 2021. That is unfathomable!

7

The Bible Says

It's time to wake up Church. It's time to push back as scripture teaches and as the Holy Spirit leads. The 1st century Church faced far greater persecution when all three worldly forces of their day— the Roman Empire, the local governments, and the local religious leaders—worked in unison to "shut them up" in effort to erase Jesus from the culture. Sound familiar?

Read the Book of Acts to see how they responded and compare the courageous acts of Peter and John and Paul and Priscilla and all the other builders of the Christian Church to the words and actions we're witnessing from most church leaders today. There's virtually no likeness, and it's heartbreaking. At this point, the Church is walking in gross disobedience to the truth of Scripture. That may sound like provocative rhetoric, but it is sadly factual.

Biblical Reasons Churches Must Open

Let me address 7 points that prove that churches should disregard the mandates, open up their buildings, pastor their people, and march on in the power of the Gospel.

1. The power is in the gathering

Jesus intentionally proved this throughout His ministry—in His words and in His daily walk. He always made it perfectly clear that gathering crowds to hear His teachings was crucial to understanding His Kingdom and to building fruitful relationships in the body of Christ. I don't know a true believer who doesn't hunger for church gatherings. It is our sanctuary, our healing place, our altar to cry on, our time to give back, our word of encouragement, our safe place for our kids to learn, our pool to be baptized, our sacred house of prayer, and above all our place to love and worship the living God and feel His power the way Jesus taught us, "as one," just as He and the Father are one! (John 17:21)

Few experiences rival being among the fellowship of believers while lifting our voices together to worship Him. THAT'S the power, and we desperately need it. The whole world needs it. You need it. Jesus said He would be right here in the midst of us whenever and wherever we gather (Mt 18:20). Why would we ever relinquish a gathering where we know we can feel His tangible presence? I can't, and our people at Global Vision Bible Church can't. Jesus died to ensure we could live and love and worship our Father in Heaven fearlessly with power from on high, just like the 1st century believers...

And they, continuing daily with one accord in the temple, and breaking bread from house to house, did eat their meat with gladness and singleness of heart, Praising God, and having favour with all the people. And the Lord added to the church daily such as should be saved.

~ Acts 2:46-47

Let's not ever again relinquish the power to gather, for it is the power to save.

2. The local church is still the pillar and ground of the truth

This is a simple Biblical fact. The Apostle Paul wrote this simple truth in his second letter to Timothy, instructing how he should conduct himself in the house of God, "which is the church of the living God, the pillar and ground of the truth" (2 Timothy 2:15). In the modern era we have the tremendous blessing of Scripture being readily available in virtually every medium imaginable. We've got it all right at our fingertips. But this doesn't replace the critical role of the local church as the ground of truth. Scripture constantly reminds us that the local church is the necessary forum to end controversies, to settle conflicts, to "rightly divide" and understand the Scripture, to seek wise counsel, to search out the mysteries of God with like-minded believers, and to train up our children in the ways of the Lord while gathered with peers of their own.

The sharing of truth in large gatherings is inspiring. And what's crazy is few of us were getting enough Bible truth before all this nonsense began. We definitely need private study, but Scripture is clear about the need for public preaching of the Word. All believers need direct access to well-trained teachers who take seriously their responsibility before God to ensure we are being fed the Word in the house of God (see James 3:1, Hebrews 13:17). Jesus is still the only way, the only truth, and the only life, and still, no one comes to the Father except through Him. If the local church isn't open, where do the lost go to talk to someone about Jesus? The liquor stores?

3. The closer we get to the coming of Christ, the more we are commanded to meet

And let us consider one another to provoke unto love and to good works: Not forsaking the assembling of ourselves together, as the manner of some is; but exhorting one another: and so much the more, as ye see the day approaching.

~ Hebrews 10:24-25

Could it be put more plainly? Surely the day of His coming is drawing near. We can't neglect our gatherings pastors, especially not in these days of lawlessness and Christian persecution. For a true believer, this is a non-negotiable. In China, the Christians risk their very lives to fulfill this beautiful exhortation and countless innocent souls have been imprisoned or executed for their faith.

More on that later. We cannot surrender our right or our need to gather just because politicians and fear mongers betray the law of the land to command our submission. Throughout the Gospels we see Jesus commending those who meet when and where He calls them, no matter the cost, and we also see Him condemning those who refuse.

Don't miss that… Jesus often condemned or severely warned those who refused to become His disciple once He called them. The negligent wedding guests of Matthew 22 and the foolish virgins of Matthew 25 are examples. Both of these foreboding parables deal with the coming of Christ, and both deal harshly with those who aren't ready when He calls them out. If we take Jesus at His word, and if we take these teachings seriously, those who make a habit of neglecting the gathering of the saints are in danger of not being ready when He comes calling again. "For many are called, but few are chosen." says the Lord. (Matthew 22:14)

4. Hell itself can't stop the Church

Jesus famously told Peter that not even the gates of hell could prevail against His Church. He also promised He would give us the keys to the Kingdom of heaven and that He would empower our prayers regarding all things in heaven and earth (Matthew 16:18-19).

The Church is His master plan. Jesus bestows this amazing promise specifically to the Church so we can wage spiritual warfare. And as we've seen, we can't fully operate as the Church if we don't gather and we risk this supernatural covering if we fail to be the Church. Every true believer who attends a living church recognizes that it is their sanctuary, not just from the troubles of the world, but from the forces of evil and darkness in the heavenly realm. Yes, Satan and his demons are very real, and they're on the move like never before, but neither he nor his minions nor his puppets in this world can prevail against the Church of Jesus Christ when we gather! We want this covering, we need this covering, and we refuse to surrender this covering no matter who acts as the devil's advocate. There's no mystery to why they want to shut us down while the darkness advances across the earth. If our local churches fail to function with the same commitment to unity and courage that Peter and the Apostles demonstrated before laying down their lives, can we really expect to retain the power Jesus promised solely to the church that was built on this rock? I don't see how anyone would risk such a promise at a time such as this.

5. The world is in desperate need of hope

Let's be honest about this. From the days Jesus walked this earth to today our faith and hope have been rooted in the unshakeable ground that is the living Church. For 2000 years we have been marked by our love, our joy, our courage, our service to the needy, and our unmatchable HOPE in the goodness of God in Christ Jesus. There's a reason that Christian churches dot the landscape all across the free world.

We as the local church are the beacon of hope to our neighbors and our communities and the lost folks down the street. In a world crippled by fear and uncertainty, hope in Christ is the only true antidote. Scripture reminds us that "hope deferred makes the heart sick" (Proverbs 13:12) and that "hope does not disappoint, because the love of God has been poured out in our hearts by the Holy Spirit who was given to us." (Romans 5:5)

How can a pastor in clear conscience before God shut the doors to the hurting, the lonely, the burdened, or the hopeless? And what of the truly lost who are desperate for answers or ready to give their life to Christ if only someone would meet and pray with them face-to-face? Let's be reminded that as pastors, the Lord holds us responsible to love and feed His flock. Right now, His flocks are starving for hope, and so are the lost. Don't deny them.

6. Pastors are called to be bold voices in a confused culture

This is about as obvious as it gets. Being a bold voice in a confused culture is pretty much the job description for a pastor, and it always has been. While we have plenty of great role models in the New Testament, several of whom we'll meet in just a bit, Jesus is the sole example of how a "good shepherd" should speak to every situation, and boldness is a prerequisite.

If you're not preaching boldly to help your flock navigate through all this confusion, you're probably in the wrong profession. Look at the Apostles of the 1st century Church. No pastor can read the Book of Acts and come away thinking we should ever bow to the dictates of lawless officials or shrink into silence when fear, confusion, deception, and darkness cover the land. Jesus said:

Ye are the salt of the earth: but if the salt have lost his savour, wherewith shall it be salted? it is thenceforth good for nothing, but to be cast out, and to be trodden under foot of men.
~ Matthew 5:13

What good is a pastor who has lost his salt? What comes of any believer who has lost his salt? Come on pastors, I know you realize what Jesus is saying here. Are you really okay with being trampled underfoot by men? Wouldn't you rather get salty and speak out? Jesus also said:

Ye are the light of the world. A city that is set on an hill cannot be hid. Neither do men light a candle, and put it under a bushel, but on a candlestick; and it giveth light unto all that are in the house. Let your light so shine before men, that they may see your good works, and glorify your Father which is in heaven.
~ Matthew 5:14-15

Are you hiding under a basket pastor? Come on out and let your light shine before men so that they may see your good works and glorify your Father in heaven. I know many of you want to speak boldly, but you fear the persecution that may come if you act on it. Be reminded that Jesus said:

Fear them not therefore: for there is nothing covered, that shall not be revealed; and hid, that shall not be known. What I tell you in darkness, that speak ye in light: and what ye hear in the ear, that preach ye upon the housetops.

~ Matthew 10:26-27

Amen?

7. God never makes an exception for the authority of the Church...

And neither does the law of this land, which is the Constitution of the United States. Look at every chapter of the New Testament from the Gospel of Matthew to the Book of Revelation and you won't find a category of Christians that gets a pass on obeying all Scripture regardless of the laws of men… and sometimes in spite of them. And our authority is established in even stronger terms in the Old Testament. In all things, the children of God are to be the head, not the tail. (Deuteronomy 28:13)

The church is never told to bow to any worldly authority. We are a blessing to all, and no faith has proven to be a greater blessing to the world than Christianity. The Judeo-Christian moral code is the bedrock of Western Civilization for good reason. It can be trusted. There is to be no authority over God's Word, least of all a lawless group of tyrants who ignore the law of the land while attempting to lord over us and diminish the authority of the Bible in our lives. According to the Constitution, we can gather peacefully wherever we'd like whenever we'd like, especially if we're a religious organization, so we're doubly protected by the 1st Amendment. Why would we abdicate that God-given, Constitutionally protected right? In a free land that's a treasured privilege, but the number of nations that honor this privilege is dwindling fast. We are to be peacemakers not pawns. We gather as the Church in obedience to God. Let no man tear us apart.

When the fearful cite Romans 13 to justify their surrender, they prove a misunderstanding or an outright misappropriation of the Scripture. First of all, it should go without saying that we are never to obey a government that commands us to do something that is sinful according to the Bible. Nothing and no one has authority over the Holy Scripture, and God will never contradict His word, nor will He ever give a man permission to ignore His word. When we do, we do so at our own peril. Second, the Lord ensured Romans 13:3 defines the type of "ruler" He would have us obey as an authority in our lives.

If an authority works against those who do good rather than those who do evil, they are in effect disqualified. So if the so-called rulers are a terror to the church doing good works, or practice the type of tyranny that shuts down these good works as we're currently experiencing, or if they praise those who do evil while threatening the Church—all against the law of the land— would the Lord ever command us to obey such lawlessness? Not a chance. We are called to be peacemakers, not pawns. Jesus alone is Lord, and the lawless have no authority over His church.

The Bottom Line
When it comes to persecution, few knew it better than the Apostles and the original body of Christ after the resurrection. Once under the influence of the Holy Spirit, the Apostles began gathering crowds and preaching Jesus boldly everywhere they went. Punishing beatings and imprisonments ensued, but the church grew leaps and bounds. Reports of the Apostles' miracles were spreading like wildfire when Peter and several of the Apostles pulled their first Houdini-like jailbreak with the help of an angel of the Lord. And rather than run away to safety, instead they headed straight back to the temple to start preaching again! How's that for bold?

What would you have done if you were in this situation? What would your pastor have done? The Apostles were immediately arrested again, and they expected no less. Then they were brought before the High Council of the Sanhedrin, the same council that condemned Jesus weeks earlier, and their dialogue addresses the Romans 13 paradox with an absolute mic drop. During the interrogation, the Chief Priest addressed Peter and the others, saying:

Did not we straightly command you that ye should not teach in this name? and, behold, ye have filled Jerusalem with your doctrine, and intend to bring this man's blood upon us. Then Peter and the other apostles answered and said, "We ought to obey God rather than men."

~ Acts 5:28-29

"We ought to obey God rather than men," ladies and gentlemen. Peter and the boys could hardly have put it more plainly. Has there ever been a more important message at a more important time? Do you think maybe in these last days God expects the same response from His disciples that He got during the first days? The Bible says there's no question about it.

8

If God Be for Us

At the climax of this historic confrontation, while the council began calling for the execution of Peter and the others for their brazen disobedience—defiantly acted out in their very courts no less—God again intervened. This time He used the Pharisee Gamaliel, an elder statesman of unrivaled respect and a true doctor of the law.

Imagine the scene in the context of the time. Don't forget this same council condemned Jesus to death just a few weeks earlier. Jerusalem was still in an uproar from the fallout of the Roman Army's mass executions of the Jews, which climaxed with the public crucifixion of Jesus.

That dark Friday left the city in a total mess. On top of all that, new converts from all over the known world were pouring into Jerusalem in response to the Holy Spirit's outpouring that had only just begun. So to say things were chaotic and explosive would be an understatement. And there was wise old Gamaliel, surely raising his hand to silence all his outraged colleagues in the Sanhedrin who were demanding Peter's head, when the old man uttered the truest words ever spoken by an unbeliever:

And now I say unto you, Refrain from these men, and let them alone: for if this counsel or this work be of men, it will come to nought: But if it be of God, ye cannot overthrow it; lest haply ye be found even to fight against God.

~ Acts 5:38-39

And they all agreed! Try to picture that scene. Peter and the others must have thought "this is it; we die this day for the sake of the Gospel." And the Holy Spirit showed up in a most unlikely Pharisee and prophesied through Him just in the nick of time. If God be for us, then who can be against us Church? No one! How can we know this bottom-line truth is the undeniable Word of God and ever respond to persecution with fear or trepidation?

Pastors, when persecution comes—even if it results in your arrest—if you believe the overarching message of this historic trial, how could you do anything but run right back into the temple to preach? Keep in mind that this was barely the beginning of the persecution for the Apostles, as even this lifesaving move of God was marked with sufferings. Let's continue reading to the end of chapter 5:

And to [Gamaliel] they agreed: and when they had called the apostles, and beaten them, they commanded that they should not speak in the name of Jesus, and let them go. And they departed from the presence of the council, rejoicing that they were counted worthy to suffer shame for his name. And daily in the temple, and in every house, they ceased not to teach and preach Jesus Christ.

~ Acts 5:40-42

So before releasing them, the Pharisees had them beaten *again*, and again they threatened them with execution if they ever preached the name of Jesus. Nonetheless, they walked out rejoicing that they were counted worthy to suffer shame for his name, and went right back to preaching in EVERY house, not just their own.

Now that's BOLD. Right now, we need some pastors and other believers to be "counted worthy" of the same. Thank God the first disciples were so courageous and faithful that they refused to cease preaching Jesus "daily in the temple and in every house," no matter the threat! Right now, most pastors aren't bold enough to suffer Facebook criticism, let alone shameful beatings, imprisonments, and death threats. Be emboldened people of God! As we continue in Acts, we read:

And in those days when the number of the disciples was multiplied, there arose a murmuring of the Grecians, against the Hebrews, because their widows were neglected in the daily administration. Then the twelve called the multitude of the disciples unto them, and said, It is not reason that we should leave the word of God, and serve tables. Wherefore, brethren, look ye out among you seven men of honest report, full of the Holy Ghost and wisdom, whom we may appoint over this business. But we will give ourselves continually to prayer, and to the ministry of the word.

~ Acts 6:1-4

In Those Days

I want you to notice the very first phrase of Acts 6:1, as I believe it sets a beautiful context and tone for all that the Apostles would do next, even as they dealt with continued persecution and divisiveness forming within their ranks. "And in those days..." Those days can best be identified as the days of great persecution, and even more, the days when the persecution brought about the very first revival.

God told these people that He wanted them to multiply and to go into all the world to preach the Gospel to every creature, red and yellow, black and white, tall and short, fat and skinny, in church and out of church. And before they could get their feet wet in the baptismal the converts were already congregating around Jerusalem in huge numbers, all while being hunted and despised by nearly every authority in the region. Why? Because all they knew to do was to go where the revival fire was burning brightest, and it always burns brightest under great pressure and persecution! Don't miss that.

Persecution and the Holy Spirit

God sent persecution because the church has always grown stronger and more powerful under persecution than it ever has under prosperity. Having said that, please know I believe that persecution can also bring prosperity. We know it's God's doing when it's accompanied by an outpouring of Holy Spirit fire that manifests in boldness, but I want you to think about something for a moment.

We've enjoyed a long run of prosperity in the American church, right? But look at the weak and anemic nature of the lukewarm brand of Christianity that we have in America, in "these" days. Not a whole lot of Holy Spirit fire, and I'm not talking about the manufactured counterfeit silliness that has plagued the nation up till 2020. That fraudulent nonsense isn't holy, it isn't of the spirit, and the smoke you see comes from a smoke machine, not the fire of God. But if you go to a country like China, where they're not allowed to freely meet and can't even read the Bible in public, you'd see Holy Spirit courage and faithfulness that rivals what we see in the 1st century Church.

The Chinese in These Days

Nothing can stop the church in China from gathering in Jesus' name, even as the persecution intensifies every year, as the underground church has exploded in the face of these mass imprisonments and public executions. The persecution is not just a COVID thing in China. They can't even preach the truth in their own homes without permission… which they never get. Did you know the underground church in China is growing more rapidly than any congregation on the face of the earth? You can be sure it's not because of Twitter and Facebook. It's because they are under severe tyranny and punishing persecution, and where there's intense persecution, there is the power of the Holy Spirit for people that will endure unto the end, just as the Bible says.

Meanwhile in Africa, many thousands of Christians are being massacred for their faith. It outrages me that the mainstream media won't even consider reporting on the massive famines across that continent, let alone these horrific acts of genocide being perpetrated by African Islamic militias who are erasing entire villages of our Christian brothers and sisters of all ages. God bless these modern-day heroes of the faith. Just one more proof that the crises sweeping the world have virtually nothing to do with race or the oppression of black people. This is simply a battle between good and evil raging around the globe.

In Those Days

Don't let that opening phrase in Acts 6 slip by you, "And in those days..." These weren't days of Skittles and rainbows and unicorn cotton candy. These were days of people dying for their faith. And let me remind you that at this point it was a brand-new faith. Seven times in the book of Acts, Christianity is called "the way" or "this way." They didn't even have a word to describe its nature, its culture, and its character, and the term "Christian" had not yet been coined. Before Jesus appeared on the scene, all these disciples knew was, *"I've got to dress a certain way, I've got to walk a certain way, I've got to talk a certain way, I've got to obey Abraham, Isaac and Jacob, I've got to obey the letter of the law of Moses, and I've got to do better, and better, and better."*

Then Jesus showed up and did for the world what none of us could do for ourselves. We're seeing that revelation striking China today with unmistakable power, and we should be inspired by their living (and dying) testimony.

"In those days," when the Gospel was still brand new, it began to infiltrate the hearts of many across the Roman Empire. Thousands of people were being saved, converts were being baptized faster than they could count them, and tents were popping up all around the region surrounding Jerusalem. Notice that Acts 6:1 doesn't say the number of the "apostles" was multiplied, it says the number of the "disciples" was multiplied, so it wasn't referring just to the twelve. This verse ensures we realize that there was a very large number of disciples following Jesus Christ at this time.

I love the word "disciples" because I love disciples. Take a good look at American Christianity, which is far too American and not enough Christianity, and you will find that there are a lot of people who talk about Jesus, but very few people who actually follow him to the ends of the earth as disciples are commanded. There are a lot of people talking about discipleship, devotion, and dedication these days, but there aren't many true-blue, dyed-in-the-wool New Testament disciples to be found.

Here are some facts about discipleship that you'd be wise to never forget. It's not fancy. It's not politically correct. It's not happy-go-lucky. It's not always encouraging, but it's always about the truth. Serving Jesus Christ will not cost you something, it will cost you everything—especially in these days.

Some folks say, *"Well, that kind of preaching bothers me, because I'm afraid that if I come to Christ I'll have to give Him everything that I possess. Is God going to take all my stuff?"*

That's a bad question. The question should never be, "is God going to take everything away from me?" The question should be, "will I give it to Him if He asked for it?"

In those days, the number of the disciples were multiplied, meaning that folks kept getting saved, the Bible kept growing, the Lord kept blessing, and supernatural things kept happening... at a multiplicative rate. The more the persecution came, the deeper the church went, and the bigger it grew.

Division

Right in the middle of all this explosive growth, what does the devil do? He throws in the monkey wrench of division in effort to destroy the newborn body of Christ (Acts 6:2). The devil has been around for a long time, but his tactics have not changed one single bit. He still aims to divide, he still aims to conquer, and he still aims to kill, steal, and destroy. Jesus came to give us life and life more abundantly, so we fear not, and realize every local church has a role in His master plan for the body of Christ.

Recall the seven points we discussed earlier. The very first Christians realized the critical role of the living and active *servant* church, and they proved all seven points through their acts of courage, obedience, and compassion. These first believers moved quickly in response to the needs in the body. Could you ever imagine Peter and the gang just closing down and sending everyone home when the council threatened them? Not a chance. They were full of the Holy Spirit, and they fully realized that the people had real questions and real sufferings and real illnesses and real demons to battle.

Peter, John, James, the Marys, and the other core leaders knew these new believers needed people to love on them and talk to them about their struggles and meet their most pressing needs, just as Jesus had done for them. Today we have believers (pastors included) that deceive themselves *and* the person they look at in the mirror (yes, both faces). They try to hide away their struggles with their "fake it till I make it" Jimmy Carter smile when all they need to be is real and raw and authentic and honest with all God made them to be. Maybe this is the real missing link in the minds of the pastors who refuse to reopen their churches. Maybe they're out of touch with the people because they're out of touch with their own issues, and we all have issues. If you don't think you have issues, then your issues have issues.

When you struggle, you've got to let someone else know, because *"there hath no temptation taken you but such as is common to man."* (1 Corinthians 10:13) So, *"Confess your faults one to another, and pray one for another, that ye may be healed. The effectual fervent prayer of a righteous man availeth much."* (James 5:16)

Don't let your temptations have their way with you. Reach out to your pastors and tell them you need them to do their job. And pastors, if you're struggling and have no one to talk to about it, please reach out to me. If I can't be there for you, I'll connect you with someone who can.

More Not Less

In Acts 6:3, we see that the Apostles' immediate solution to the mounting divisions was to select *"seven men of honest report, full of the Holy Ghost and wisdom, whom we may appoint over this business."* These seven men were in effect the first care pastors and ministry leaders in church history, as their primary job was to pastor the families and people through these struggles and to lead them into total unity within the body. I know some folks think of preaching first and preaching last when we think of pastors and other church leaders, but the shepherding role of a pastor is equally critical. And in these days of COVID, don't tell me a Zoom call is an effective replacement.

Our modern communications technologies are valuable tools, but they can never replace the invaluable face-to-face, hug-a-neck, hand-in-hand ministry that happens when two or more are gathered in the name of the Lord. We need more engagement these days, not less. Likewise, while mass participation in outdoor worship gatherings can be a beautiful and powerful part of revival, they will never be able to fill the day-to-day human needs that only the local church can provide. So if you're a rally hopper, enjoy the outpouring and get your fill, but be sure to go home and ensure you pour the overflow into your local church leaders. They need it.

The First Martyr

If we continue reading through Acts, we learn that the first person assigned to this seven-man team of pastors and ministry leaders was Stephen, "a man full of faith and of the Holy Ghost." The Bible tells us that Stephen wasn't solely a ministry leader working in the tents and kitchens and storehouses and pastures to shepherd and feed the people, he was also a fiery preacher of the boldest order. Despite being fairly new to the ministry and relatively young, Stephen was so "full of faith and of the Holy Ghost" that his bold public preaching led him to becoming the very first martyr for Jesus not long after he signed up. His amazing testimony should preach to you—especially those of you relatively new to the faith. And it's so like God to ensure Stephen was executed by the Pharisees with Saul Paulus of Tarsus presiding over his stoning.

Though Saul (a disciple of Gamaliel) would gain infamy as the most feared Christian killer during the birth of the early church, he was eventually transformed into the boldest preacher, pastor, writer, and church planter in the history of the world—the man best known as the Apostle Paul. Having a Pauline encounter with the living Christ will cause that kind of radical born again conversion even in the most hardened sinners among us. I know several modern day Pauls. They're dangerous for the Gospel.

Imagine the impact Stephen's bold fiery preaching must have had on Paul's ministry as an Apostle, and Stephen wasn't even one of the front-line preachers! You've got to believe Stephen's "Holy Spirit" fearlessness in the face of death somehow emboldened Paul to stand with the same courage through all the near death stonings and beatings he survived before walking to his own execution 30 years later in Rome.

Maybe you can identify with Stephen or Paul. We know Paul often reflected on his role in Stephen's death, and few knew better than Paul exactly how the Lord works all things together for our good, so he welcomed the absolute forgiveness that came from receiving Jesus and the Holy Spirit. What about us? I'm praying for the modern-day Stephens to rise up in massive numbers so maybe more Pauls will break free from the dark spirit that's holding them back and walk into their calling, full of Holy Ghost fire.

Afraid of the Spirit?

Of course, Stephen wasn't alone among these upstart ministry leaders, as each of these were men of good reputation and—watch this—full of the Holy Ghost. I can sense someone out there thinking, *"Oh, my goodness, brother Locke… that kind of makes me nervous… I get scared when the Bible starts talking about the Holy Spirit."* Well right there in the Bible He's called the Holy Ghost, so BOO!

Seriously, don't ever be spooked by the supernatural. We're talking about the Spirit of Christ dwelling within you. You want that, right? Listen, I grew up in a denominational hierarchy where the mere mention of the Holy Ghost in Scripture made them want to take that verse plumb out of the Bible. I was often warned not to mention anything about the movement of the Spirit. Not anymore.

Jesus in the Closet

It reminds me of the little boy that got in trouble one day for doing something silly at school. So his mom thought that she would put him in timeout when he got home, but she decided to put him in a dark closet so he would learn his lesson in a shorter amount of time, and she knew he hated the dark so she figured she'd work on bringing an end to that foolishness at the same time.

It was sort of a "two birds with one stone" retribution. So she took Junior and she put him in the closet and before she shut the door she said, "now Junior, I'm going to put you in this closet for 30 minutes for your time out, but don't be afraid and don't freak out because, I want to remind you, no matter how dark it gets, Jesus is in here with you." So she shut the door tight and used a towel to cover the crack, which made it dark as a dungeon. Then she leaned over up against the door and stayed just to make sure he didn't lose it in there.

After 15 minutes or so, she heard Junior start talking to himself, and he said, *"now, Lord Jesus, I know you're in this closet with me. But whatever you do, don't you dare move because you will scare me absolutely to death if you do!"*

And that's like a lot of churches today. *"Oh Lord, don't move! Don't really save anybody! We might have to go past 12 o'clock and we've got to beat the Methodists to the Chinese buffet! I know we've been praying for revival but don't send it today! I've gotta record my show this afternoon and I don't want to get stuck in the parking lot!"*

That's what I love about our Sunday services under the tent. Their cars are so blocked in that if they try to leave before I'm done preaching, they can't get out of the parking lot!

Kingdom Business

So the Bible tells us these men were full of the Holy Ghost. The Bible continually says that as an outpouring of the Holy Ghost happens, "they had boldness... they had boldness... they had boldness!" And when they prayed, they prayed for more boldness! Friends, this should be even more true today! Why are we supposed to be bold? Because those who are filled with the Holy Spirit are always bold.

When Jesus said, "I must be about my Father's business," He's talking about Kingdom business and Kingdom mindedness. You see, we've got to work while it's yet day, because the night comes when no man can work. My Paw Paw used to say, "make hay while the sun shines." We've got to do it now. And everyone's like, *"you know, 20 years from now, it'll all pan out, and I'll serve the Lord."*

If you're not serving God in 20 minutes, you won't be serving God in 20 years. It doesn't start later. It doesn't start when you get a car. It doesn't start when you graduate. It doesn't start when you get married. It doesn't start when you turn 50 or 65. It starts right now ladies and gentlemen.

The Bible says we've got to appoint these people over the Kingdom we've got to appoint these people over the business of the work of the Lord. And we need to be faithful with the ministry that God has given us. That's exactly why we never closed our doors one time during this whole thing. Because this isn't Greg's church this is God's church. In the same way, the location we use to gather has nothing to do with the blessing. It is through the act of gathering whereby we get the blessing. "Foresake not the assembling of yourselves together (Hebrews 10:25)."

9

What Happens in Vegas

A few weeks ago, my wife and I and a couple of our guys from the church flew out to Las Vegas. I was there for an Evangelicals for Trump rally and I was also there for a conference where I preached. Some of you saw that we also spent time ministering to the social media influencers, the Hodge Twins, and making some podcasts and videos with Kevin and Keith. My wife Tai and I were also guests on a Christian Television Network talk show, so it was a beautifully fruitful two-day trip. But can you guess what convicted me most while we were out there? During the rally on our first night there, 800 people showed up at a Casino hotel in the heart of Las Vegas, even though most of the town was completely shut down by all the mandates.

We were at the O'Hearn Hotel, and it was really nothing more than a giant worship service. Just as is the case in most of the US, all the churches in Las Vegas and the rest of Nevada were shut down by the unconstitutional mandates (all, that is, except the one I preached at on the second night…those were some super bold people). The mandates are absolutely ridiculous in Las Vegas. Everywhere we went there were signs reading "No mask, no service" or "No shoes, no shirt, no mask, no service." You might say, "oh brother Locke, that ain't no big deal." Yeah, and one day it will be *no shoes, no shirt, no mask, no vaccine, no mark, no service.* I'm telling you; it's coming soon. If you don't believe that you aren't paying attention.

Church in a Casino

Picture 800 people sitting at round banquet tables in a massive hotel lobby at this Evangelicals for Trump rally while the rest of the city (aside from the casinos and a few other "essential" businesses) was lifeless. The prophetic symbolism was undeniable. Five minutes before it started, a representative from the Las Vegas Mayor's office came to the event and handed the executive of the event a "cease and desist" letter, threatening that they were going to sue the owners and were going to take away their business license if they didn't shut it down immediately. Keep in mind, this is a massive Casino Convention Center in the heart of Las Vegas, and they were being told they would lose their business license if they pressed forward with this Trump rally. We already know how different it would have been if BLM or Antifa was holding the rally, but I'll try not to digress. The Mayor's justification was that they considered it to be a worship service, and worship services like this were banned in Las Vegas due to mandates. Unbelievable.

We were all sitting in there, not even really knowing what's going on behind the scenes, but it was clear by the commotion at the main entrance that something was going down. It turns out that the Convention Center owners called their lawyers and they were scrambling like helicopters all over the place until finally they decided they were just going to pay whatever they had to pay in fines and do whatever they had to do to press on because they knew God told them to have this rally, come what may.

Get Me the President

And that's about the time Donald Trump got on the line. And he was like, *look, if you stay in with me, we'll pay the legal fees. You just go ahead and do what needs to be done.* You can imagine the fire this put into their resolve. There's no denying it was a worship service. The preaching was red-hot, and we worshipped and prayed throughout the rally. I've never seen anything like it. They pushed through all the threats and intimidation with amazing calm despite the place reaching full capacity, and it was a beautiful gathering that served its purpose, and more. Let me tell you why that's important. I don't care what you believe about Donald Trump, and he's not the point. The point is, I find it sad and insane that a casino in Las Vegas was forced to risk everything including their business license and potential millions in revenue to hold a worship service. A casino venue in the world's most infamous gambling town. I don't gamble, but I can't help but appreciate those people. Think about it.

A Las Vegas casino operation plainly said, *"Bring it on. We'll take any lawsuit and legal punishment you throw down on us."* Wow. Meanwhile, 95% of the churches in America lack the conviction to be as bold as a casino, much less a living church! No church that is bowing to this lawlessness can possibly consider itself to be alive or full of the Holy Spirit. I'll step out and say that any church that bows to these lawless mandates and legal threats is shirking the call of God and their faith is dead (James 2:26). I know that will upset a lot of folks, but you picked up the wrong book if you were expecting me to write like Joel Osteen. I can promise you that.

About Compliance

I don't often carry a mask around with me. If you wear one for health reasons, praise God for you, that's cool. I'm not going to shame you for wearing one, so please don't shame me for not. I don't care if it chaps the hide of the devil, so hear me well. People have immune deficiencies. I get it, and I'm glad that you are health conscious. I'm not going to get up in your face with bad breath and spit on you. But if you think masks are about safety, you have lost your mind. The real science proves masks do more harm than good, so this isn't about safety, it's about compliance. This is about compliance and nothing but compliance! I know most of you agree, but you can trust that I'd say that even if you didn't agree. I'm done with this nonsense, and this is God's business we're doing, so we're not going to let a casino be a bolder church than the Church! We're not going to let a casino out-God us. We're not going to let a casino out-conviction us. This is God's business. And I'm telling you, it's going to get a whole lot worse before it gets better.

Pleasing the Whole Multitude

In case you think Peter and the rest of the twelve were suddenly taking long sabbaticals and letting folks like Stephen do all the hard work, take a look at Acts 6:4-5. The passage reads, "But we [the Apostles] will give ourselves continually to prayer, and to the ministry of the Word. This saying pleased the whole multitude."

When reading Acts chapter 6 it's pretty clear that the Apostles weren't really concerned about what the crowds wanted them to do, but you know it had to be an especially encouraging confirmation to know the multitudes of new believers were fully on board with their leadership. If you would like to see your pastor please the whole multitude this way, challenge them to boldly take on the Apostle's convictions as displayed in these early chapters of Acts, and remind them they can't do this while shut away in their home or hiding in their church office while the front doors are locked.

As we continue in Acts 6:5-6, we learn the names of the seven original ministry leaders and see that the Apostles laid hands on them and prayed for them. As commonplace as that seems, don't zoom past this passage without remembering the importance of human contact—especially the laying of hands—when praying power and healing into people.

Is it really so easy to believe we can properly engage in this spiritual war without maintaining the spiritual weapons like the laying of hands in prayer? Not a chance. You can't lay hands through a Zoom call. Yet even in the face of great persecution, and in part because of the persecution, we see in verse seven that the Kingdom of God advanced in every way.

The Word of God Increased

*"And the word of God increased; and the number of the disciples
multiplied in Jerusalem greatly; and a great company of the priests
were obedient to the faith." And the word of God increased.*

~ *Acts 6:7*

When they stayed faithful during the persecution, as the revival
was blowing up all around them, as they were reading and
preaching and praying and fasting, the Word of God increased.
That's all I want. Even the pastors at home with shut down
churches will say that's all they want. But we're seeing a decrease
in the Word of God because men and women of God are
abandoning their posts. I want to see an increase in the Word of
God. I want to see more people come to the Kingdom. I want to
see more people get saved, more people get baptized, more
marriages restored, and more people's lives turned around. I want
to see the Word of God increase, not decrease. And if we want to
see the Word of God increase, then we have to decrease, just as
John the Baptist said, "He must increase and I must decrease," so
that in all things He might have the preeminence.

Jesus cannot merely be a name in the Church, He has to be
in control. "And the Word of God increased..." That's what I want
to see—a hunger in the Church for the Word of God like never
before. No matter who's preaching and teaching, I pray for people
to kill their addictions to personalities—especially their own—and
I pray instead they become addicted to the truth of Christ through
increased consumption of the Word of God.

A Great Company of Priests
Acts 6:7 is one of the most overlooked verses in the whole book of
Acts, especially in the context of the story. This is a beautiful
phrase. I want to tell you the gravity, the weight, the severity of

such a phrase. After all these people are saved, after all these disciples are multiplied greatly, it says, "And a great company (not a handful, not a dozen, but a great company) of the priests were obedient to the faith." You know why that's important? The priests were the most religiously and denominationally supercharged people in the whole Bible. These were the people that protected and enforced the law to the very letter. These were the most religious people in the church. These were the people that had been trained in seminary to obey the law but knew nothing about the truth of the life-giving liberating power of the Gospel of Jesus Christ.

They knew about the Old Testament, but they rejected the blood of Jesus. Yet this "great company of the priests" suddenly got born again. That's revival. And all the while, this movement came through the back door of strict and severe persecution. So much was happening right before their eyes that not even the priests could deny the life giving the power of the Gospel.

A great company of hardened religious denominational hierarchy leaders got born again by the grace of God because they could not deny the power of God that was on full display. There was so much power of God and presence of the Holy Spirit blowing through the streets of Jerusalem that even the hyper-religious people were losing their facades and getting born again.

I know I fuss about masks and rant about masks, but do you know why this sudden masking of America and its general acceptance doesn't really surprise me? Because I've been preaching for 28 years to people who wear masks, and the symbolism doesn't escape me. Please don't let it escape you. The church is full of mask-wearing wannabe Christians—fake folks only fooling themselves. Everyone needs to know that when you're born again, there will be a definite transformation of your heart. "Old things are passed away; behold, all things become new." (2 Corinthians 5:17) When you truly get born again, you don't get permission to live any way you want to, and you don't want it.

You get the honor of submitting to the will of God. That's Bible salvation. That's what it means to repent and believe the Gospel. You don't gain a free pass to sin or to shirk your calling, you gain the heavenly right to submit to the Lordship of Jesus Christ. "And a great company of the priests were obedient to the faith." They saw something real, and they could not deny its reality.

A Good Time for Scoffers

To outsiders, it looks like Christians are trying to convince the world to believe something that Christians don't even believe. We're trying to peddle something to the world that the church in America doesn't even believe, let alone practice. We talk about faith. We talk about the healing. We talk about how God is all powerful. And then we see 95 to 98 percent of the churches willingly shut down because, apparently, God can't heal, and there's no real faith, and there is no power, and there is no presence of the Spirit, so no big loss. Is that it?

All of a sudden, churches have surrendered everything that we preach and succumbed to everything we preach against, and the world says, "Ah, see, we knew it was gonna happen! We knew they'd cower in fear just like the rest of us! They're no more powerful than we are!" Let's be honest. The church landscape in America has forever been changed. That's not a prophecy, that's not a prediction, that's just a fact. It has forevermore been changed, and it will never again be the same. And this reveals the reason why God is allowing this present persecution. He's thinning out the ranks, so he can raise up an army of Peters and Stephens and Marys and Pauls and Pricillas. May we be that generation where multitudes are reached, and multitudes stand up like a mighty army.

We're not going to capitulate to the culture. We're not going to roll over. We're going to be bold, and we're going to preach, and we're going to fast and we're going to sing, and we're going to worship, and we're going to stay open, and we are not going to take a knee, and we are not going to bow, and we are not going to close up shop, and we are not going to lock the doors. We're going to call perversity, perversity, and we're going to call righteousness, righteousness, and we're going to reach hurting people, because that is who God called us to be. May we be found faithful in these days of chaos.

Closing Prayer

May we be found faithful in these days of chaos and all of God's people see it. Father, thank you today for the glory of God under this tent. Thank you for the preached word of the living God and for the power of this book we call the Bible. It's undeniable. God gave us boldness. God, I pray if nothing else, that you'll help us to realize that Christianity in our culture has in fact become weak and anemic and powerless. It's come to a place where people don't even believe what we say anymore. But I believe when people see something that's real, see something that's in action, and know that faith without works is dead, and know that You're still working in some pockets and wonderful places all over the nation... where there are people that haven't given up, people that haven't given in, people that saw it for what it was. Lord, I believe people are drawn to a place like that. This know also, that in the last days perilous, dangerous, evil, corrupt times shall come. Keep us in Your will oh Lord. Give us a Holy hunger. Give us a Holy hunger and a passionate Holy Spirit boldness to cut through the nonsense of this culture and call it what it is and stand up. Because as long as you are pleased, nothing else matters. Nothing else. In the precious and powerful name of Jesus we pray, amen.

Part III: Preparation

"And he shall send his angels with a great sound of a trumpet, and they shall gather together his elect from the four winds, from one end of heaven to the other. Now learn a parable of the fig tree; When his branch is yet tender, and putteth forth leaves, ye know that summer is nigh: So likewise ye, when ye shall see all these things, know that it is near, even at the doors. Verily I say unto you, This generation shall not pass, till all these things be fulfilled. Heaven and earth shall pass away, but my words shall not pass away. But of that day and hour knoweth no man, no, not the angels of heaven, but my Father only. But as the days of Noah were, so shall also the coming of the Son of man be." ~Jesus

Matthew 24:31-37

10

The Dawn of Revival

When the Coronavirus lockdown on churches was first instituted in Tennessee, many of our church family reached out to me to ensure I planned to remain open, and while I was greatly inspired by their conviction, I wasn't surprised. Our people love Jesus like crazy, and I'm sure few among them thought for one second I would fail to continue gathering. Come hell or high water, I have to obey the word of God and I live to preach the Gospel, so what else is there? In the months since, we've gone from small indoor gatherings in our sanctuary to drive-in services in the parking lot to the large revival tent we're currently using as our primary gathering place. Through it all, I've been amazed by the exponential growth of our family, both under the tent and online by way of our live streams.

The Lord began using us to spark a global movement in 2015 and then supercharged us during the 2016 election season, and we have folks who drive or fly in for our services from all across the nation, so we've long known He was doing something different with us. Some even fly in from other countries, which is finally starting to make sense. When we decided to name our church Global Vision Bible Church all those years ago, only God could have known what would happen here. I'm honored to serve all who have joined our growing family through four stormy years, even more so during these long-awaited days.

It truly is amazing what God is doing, and I thank Him for the privilege to pastor a group of people who are willing to be bold and willing to be brave. I am convinced that courage is contagious, especially in these last days, and I'm deeply moved by all of you who have found your voice and have chosen to stand firm. I would preach the way I preach even if our people were throwing tomatoes at me, because we're living in days when people just need to straighten up and be bold for Jesus Christ.

It Starts with a Breath

People call us all the time asking, "What are you guys doing to draw such crowds?" The answer is simple. We're just preaching the Bible and loving on each other. Others ask why people keep coming even though we're meeting in a tent out in the summer heat, and I ask myself that same question every single weekend. I don't know all the reasons why the Lord is doing what He's doing but you can be sure that He's the one doing it. Our job is to be faithful with it. Some believe we're at the dawn of a great revival… the revival that so many have prayed would break out in 2020. People of God around the world have long been speaking of Nashville being an epicenter when it all breaks out and sweeps across this nation and around the globe. Maybe they're right.

Others share their doubts about the possibility of a true revival ever breaking out in these dark days. I see their point too. With the lack of courage and the absence of true repentance we're witnessing by most pastors, preachers, and priests in America, it's a logical conclusion. But in the face of all the dark forces we're seeing at work in every corner of our culture, we need these men and women of God more today than ever.

The enemy is trying to strip Christianity out of the public forum while dismantling the Judeo-Christian moral code that is the cornerstone of this great nation. They have chosen to start a culture war against everything we hold most dear. And since this is without question a spiritual war between good and evil, we'd better get prepared for the battles at hand, as fast as we can. Can God breathe life into a dying church, and if so, how? The answer is found in the prophetic life of Ezekiel, "Son of man," in what is possibly the most important prophetic vision in the entire Bible—especially as it relates to the here and now.

Opening Prayer

Before we dive into the text of this section, please pray this simple prayer with me. Heavenly Father, I come to you as humbly as I can, and I ask that you use this message deep in our hearts. Lord, I pray that you will do what Greg Locke cannot do. We need the Holy Spirit to do a work in us that humanly speaking must be supernatural... to do something exceedingly abundantly above all we could ever ask or think. And, Lord, we are not so naive to believe that we accidentally bebopped into the Scripture we'll explore in this section. Surely, You've drawn us to this text for such a time as this. I pray that you would break our hearts, You would bend our knees, You would embolden our voices and strengthen our backbones. Bless what we're about to discover as we pray, in the mighty name of Jesus, amen.

Ezekiel's Stunning Prophetic Vision

In Ezekiel chapter 37 we find a very unusual passage that prophetically addresses revival in the most visually powerful way imaginable. As we take a look into Ezekiel's stunning revelation, I want to share how I was led to making the prophecy a central theme in this book.

On a recent Sunday morning, the Lord jolted me right up out of bed even though I was exhausted from an especially busy week. I had just returned from an outdoor crusade in Somerset, Kentucky and had been working long hours at Global Vision to increase our outdoor seating capacity and to expand our parking situation while still counseling folks and leading our staff and making time to be a good husband and father to my wife and our six kids. I was feeling exhausted and knew I was running on fumes, so I intended to sleep in a little bit later on this particular morning. God had other plans, and though I truly try to get enough sleep, I like it even more when God suddenly changes things.

It was super early, and the sun had not yet risen when BAM, the Lord just woke me up, and due to all that was racing through my mind I knew I wouldn't be able to go back to sleep. Most who know me are aware that there is a nearby tree off the beaten path that has become the most special place in the world to me. For several years now I have been visiting this tree whenever I felt the Lord calling me to seek Him in complete solitude, absent any form of distraction. This was clearly one of those times, so I got up and drove to the trail. As I was walking to the tree, I said, "Lord, I just pray you will show me this morning what you want me to tell your people today... what you want me to tell the world... what you want me to tell the folks that are going to be under our tent in just a few hours. As the tree came into view, the closer and closer I got, the stronger this realization struck me. We're living in such lukewarm days that the church has become as dry as cracker juice, and preachers and pastors are either too afraid, or simply unwilling to boldly stand up for God and His children in these troubling times.

The Lord revealed to me that even the people who are defying the orders to shut down church gatherings are scared and sheepish and increasingly afraid as they step out into this increasingly chaotic and violent world. In that moment, the Lord directed me to Ezekiel chapter 37 and said, *"I want you to preach about prophesying to the dry bones... can these bones live?"*

As I prayed in the spirit at the tree I thought, Lord, I really don't want to preach on Ezekiel 37. I don't feel very prophetic this morning. But while I was walking away and going back to my car, I knew that I had to obey what the Holy Spirit had spoken no matter what my brain was thinking.

The Restoration of Israel
I need you to know that I am absolutely aware—pastorally, theologically, and expositionally—exactly what Ezekiel chapter 37 deals with. I know that in the immediate context in which the Holy

Spirit placed it, the Lord is referring to the regathering of the nation of Israel, which is twofold. First, much of this chapter was prophetically fulfilled in 1948 when Israel was finally restored as a nation and returned to their historic homeland.

Just in case anyone doubts the fact that the land of Israel belongs to the Jewish nation, you need to get your nose out of the newspapers and stick it in the Bible. As I inferred in chapter 3, the Bible is the title and deed that proves the Holy Land belongs to the nation of Israel, and it just so happens to be the most archaeologically verified and historically trusted document concerning the ancient Middle East up to the days of Christ and the Apostles. For that, we should thank God that we have an American President who moved our embassy into the heart of Jerusalem to further validate this fact. It's also inspiring that this bold move points to directly to the prophetic nature of Scripture for all to see.

Regardless of the controversies springing up around Israel in these days, you'd better not close your eyes. Not only is Israel becoming the breadbasket of the world, the Bible tells us that all who bless Israel will be blessed. But if we dare turn against the nation of Israel, you'd better know that God will turn against us. (Genesis 12:3) If you don't believe that, you don't believe a thimble full of the Bible.

Second, Ezekiel chapter 37 also points to the day we will see with our own eyes that God is not yet done with the nation of Israel. I LOVE Israel and the Jewish people, so stick with me while I write some facts in simple terms. In their rebellion against the Gospel, those of us who were not born into Israel can be grafted in as citizens by the grace of God. He came unto his own, and his own received him not, but as many as received him, to them he gave power to become the sons of God. (John 1:11-12)

The reason gentiles are born again by the grace of the Gospel is because Israel, in part, has been blinded to the truth of Jesus Christ. But one day they will look upon Him whom they have pierced, and the entire nation of Israel will be born again in a single day.

Momentum to prepare the way is already building, as Messianic Jewish communities (Jews who have accepted Jesus and believe the Gospel) are already springing up all over the world. So never forget that God is not done with the Jewish people, and He is not done with the nation of Israel. The very week before I began writing this chapter, a truly historic peace treaty was signed between Israel and a group of influential Arab nations, and other Arab nations are sure to follow suit. This isn't one of those old-fashioned "enjoy it while it lasts" cease-fire treaties. It's not perfect, but it's a legitimate partnership that legitimizes Israel as the sole superpower in the Middle East. That's a first. The treaty also has all the markings of the permanent breakthrough in Arab-Israeli cooperation—a breakthrough most of the world thought would never ever happen. President Donald Trump brokered it all in the midst of the most complex global coup attempt in the history of Western Civilization and was rightly nominated for the Nobel Peace Prize. The Globalists will likely do all they can to block him from receiving the honor, and I'm sure he'll embrace the hate for what it is... persecution for doing the work of the Lord.

Here we are, celebrating the reality of what seemed impossible just weeks ago, and even among those of us celebrating this historic act, no one really saw it coming. We are living in days where Bible prophecy is literally jumping off the page,—pop, pop, POP!—as even the daily newspapers are proving the word of God in their newsprint. Let's hope the liberal (mostly atheist) media is getting a little bit nervous about all this. They could use a little truth serum.

Eyes that See, Ears that Hear
People still say, "I don't know if I can believe the Bible." With all we've seen since the nation of Israel was restored in 1948—after 2000 years of exile, let alone what we're witnessing in these epic

days—even hardened atheists are starting to realize all these alignments of Biblical prophecy cannot be ignored. That's why they're starting to lash out at Christians and Jews alike with such hate and deception. They're terrified of all the implications, and rightly so. Revival is at hand.

As I revisit Ezekiel 37, I'm also reminded that everything that has happened in the nation of Israel is a prophetic message to the church of the living God right now. Do I believe in Divine interpretation? Yes, but I also believe that the Bible is a book of application. I am convinced that what we see in this passage of Ezekiel is not just referring to the Jews, but also to every single person in the body of Christ today. These are the days where the modern church is literally being called out in the Word of God. Let's pray the lost and the lukewarm are paying attention.

For this people's heart is waxed gross, and their ears are dull of hearing, and their eyes they have closed; lest at any time they should see with their eyes and hear with their ears, and should understand with their heart, and should be converted, and I should heal them. ~Jesus

Matthew 13:15

11

Can Dry Bones Live?

"The hand of the Lord was upon me, and carried me out in the spirit of the Lord, and set me down in the midst of the valley which was full of bones"

~ Ezekiel 37:1

Ezekiel Chapter 37 verse one starts off by saying, "The hand of the Lord was upon me..." We need to stop and hitch our trailer to that part of the verse, because if that's not true of your life, you're not going to get one thing out of what I say in this book. If you're reading this to learn for Greg Locke, you picked up the wrong book at the wrong time. All is in vain unless the Spirit of the Holy One comes down and speaks directly to you through these pages. I have some heroes and I have some people I admire, but I don't suffer from an ounce of man worship. I'm too full of Jesus-worship to make room for any of that idolatry, and I want the Spirit of God to be upon me whether I'm speaking or writing or reading or just moving through my day.

I don't want to preach microwave sermons, I don't want to write microwave books, and I don't want to sing microwave songs. Sometimes we read the Bible or go to church because it's the thing to do. The alarm goes off, we hit snooze 55 times, we get our coffee, we come rolling up to the church, we've been screaming at the kids, we've been screaming at our spouse, and we get out of the car with a Jimmy Carter smile expecting God to bless us. No more. I want the hand of God to be upon this preacher. I want His hand to be upon our church and upon our livestream viewers and upon you right now as you read this. When I get into people's presence, I want them to say, "there is a man who seeks the face of God!" That's all that matters. So ask Him again to keep His hand on you as He downloads His word to you in the coming chapters, and I'm confident you will receive what you ask for.

God Still Speaks

Returning to verse one we read, "The hand of the Lord was upon me, and carried me out in the spirit of the Lord and set me down in the midst of the valley which was full of bones." It was full of death. It was full of stench. It was full arrogance. It was full of ungodliness. It was full of self-righteousness—a valley full of bones. I love how it says Ezekiel went out "in the spirit." If the hand of God is upon you and the Spirit of God is leading you, He will take you to the right place at the right time and the only thing that stands between you and God's blessing, is YOU. So you'd better get out of God's way and let Him speak. You'd better let Him do what He wants to do in your life.

I tell my people all the time, for a guy like me that grew up "Baptist born and Baptist bread and when I die I'd be Baptist dead," I have to admit I never thought in a million worlds that I'd walk away from the Baptist denomination as I did some years ago. In my life, such a move was like sinking the Titanic, praise God. That's not a slam against Baptists of course. I'm grateful for my roots and I still preach in Baptist churches all the time, so I love Baptists as much today as I ever have. But I also admit that for years of my ministry I would say things like, "Well, you know, God doesn't speak other than how I've been taught that He speaks...the Spirit of God doesn't do this or that... I don't know about all that healing business... I don't know about all these people having dreams in the night, etc."

But that was then, and this is now. It's worth repeating again and again… if a revelation or supernatural act doesn't contradict what the Word of God says, I prefer to believe it. I'm seeing and hearing God do and say some amazing things with my own eyes and ears. Even if I was formerly a cessationist—the theological term for someone who believes the supernatural gifts of the Spirit "ceased" when the original Apostles left the scene—or even if I still believed that, I know what the Bible says. In the last days, God will pour out His Spirit upon all men, and your old men will dream dreams, and your young men will see visions, and people will prophesy (Acts 2:17). I can't deny the fact that when God's Spirit shows up, He doesn't need my permission or anyone else's to do His work, and we should be eager to receive all He reveals and pours out in this season.

Dry Bones

And [the Spirit] caused me to pass by them round about: and, behold, there were very many in the open valley; and, lo, they were very dry.

~ *Ezekiel 37:2*

Recall that the Spirit of God carried Ezekiel into the valley that was "full of bones." The bones were absolutely everywhere. Then verse two says the bones "were very dry." Let me say right here that this has become the distinguishing characteristic of most American churches in these dark days. They are very dry. DRY. Absolutely no power. No fire. No excitement. Roll in, roll out. Don't go longer than an hour. Clock in on God's clock, clock out on God's clock. Don't preach too long. Don't baptize too many people. Don't pray too long. Don't talk about the offering too long. Don't sing an extra stanza of the song. Most churches strive to ensure their visitors and members are comfortable. Personally, I like to keep people in church long enough that they get uncomfortable, and I'm starting to see how God is using discomfort to help us realize that the Church in America has indeed become dry and lifeless as we bask in our comfort.

Turning Up the Heat

During the dog days of summer in our COVID-era revival tent it's already 5000 degrees so our people are already good and uncomfortable. I figure they might as well stick around, and we might as well keep it real and stay uncomfortable because we don't grow in our comfort zone anyway. Sometimes we get a little bit too cozy on our plush couches, and we get a bit too relaxed with our online worship, and we like our nice little padded pews and padded chairs in our spacious sanctuaries.

We've got an air conditioner blowing up our pants leg on a hot day and it's all so comfortable. We've got high-tech redneck video screens and surround sound all over the place. It's cool. Yet here's what God does in all His glory and all of His sovereignty. He decides He's going to kick the lid off of the whole thing and put us outside during the hottest summer on record in Middle Tennessee. That's not a joke. The hottest summer ever. And then He filled up our tent, kept on adding more chairs, turned up the heat in more ways than one, and got people fanning themselves with funeral home fans, and not a single complaint is ever heard. Folks are still getting saved, people are still getting right, converts are still getting baptized, and things are still happening beyond our wildest expectations. But here's what I'm finding as I crisscross America. Most churches are happy being comfortably complacent. Some are saying, "well, you know, Pastor Locke, we don't want to rock the boat too much." I'm counting on it.

More Not Less

I am so past caring what people think about me and our church in the media. I'm over it. I couldn't care less. It's gotten to the point that I expect to wake up to critical news articles. I expect people to get mad. I expect the protesters to show up when we have Roger Stone giving his salvation testimony. We'll give them water and tell them about Jesus. I'm not the least bit worried about it. We're not going to stop. We are not going to give up and we are not going to give in. We are going to be bolder than we have ever been. If you think we've stirred up some trouble lately, stay tuned. We haven't even started yet!

Dry bones, that's where we are in the American church. Dry bones. The same people who say, "don't get too loud preacher," will go to a ballgame and scream their lungs out, begging for double overtime. You've got to be at work the next day but "oh my goodness I'll stay till two in the morning if my team's winning!" Did you know that if the average Christian gave their boss the same excuse for not going to work that they give God and the pastor for not going to church, He would have fired your tail six months ago? Do you remember what the Bible says in Hebrews 10:25? *"Not forsaking the assembling of ourselves together, as the manner of some is; but exhorting one another: and so much the more, as ye see the day approaching."* Yes! "So much the more!"

The Dry Church
Did you know the closer we get to the coming of Christ, the drier people's faith is going to become? But for the bold few, our faith is going to become more exciting. That's what we need to be. We need to gather more, we need to be in church more, we need to fast more, pray more, worship more, sing more, give more, and get to the altar more. God didn't say to do it less. He says to do it more. But what do we have now? We have churches all over America on lockdown. I hope you haven't grown numb to that fact. I'm still in a state of unbelief.

I love that Dr. John MacArthur and some others have started to push back out west. They are fighting in the courts against the godless state of California, and all they had to do was stand up and fight back to be obedient to God. What about the rest of us? The government knows they don't have a leg to stand on because they don't have a constitutional right to shut our churches... unless we let them. That's all well and good but here's where the other shoe falls. When McArthur's team initially won temporary "permission" to open on a particular weekend, 90% of the churches in California still remained closed by choice! That's not a governmental problem, that's a church-pastor problem. That's a coward problem. That's a no-backbone problem.

We have people driving in from all over to join our worship services under our tent because their church is still shut down. God bless all our visitors who are traveling in and joining us to lift up the name of Jesus every Sunday, but I exhort each to go back to their hometown and let their pastor know that Pastor Locke says, "Shame on you man of God for not opening your church when it should be open!" This is ridiculous.

Who Needs a Revival?

The government is telling us when we can meet and when we can't meet. You know why the Church is going along with it? Because the Church is dry. Colder than *a mother-in-law's kiss*. No revival. No Holy Spirit power. The Church is freaked out that God is going to show up and do something different, because the average church in America can't even function without a bulletin. We know when to stand, we know when to sit, we know when to give, we know when to be greedy, we know when to come in, we know when to go out, we know when to sing this, we know when to say that, we know when to amen, we know when to "oh me." When it's all said and done, the American Church shows up and has church whether God shows up or not, and that stinks in God's holy nostrils.

If we've ever needed a revival, we need it right this very moment. I believe it's coming. I believe we're on the edge of it. I believe it is here. And I think it's coming through the back door of persecution. But the only churches that are going to experience this move of God are the ones that are willing to get up, open the doors, risk persecution, and refuse to miss what the Holy Ghost is doing in this nation in these final days.

A Church Alive

I could give you a long list of reasons churches are dry, but you've been in enough of them to know it's true. I'm not saying you have to have standing ovations. I'm not saying you even have to clap. I'm not saying you have to hoot and holler and run to the altar. But you can tell when you go to a church that is alive and when you go to a church that is as dead and lukewarm as the church of Laodicea in the Book of Revelation.

There's a reason people fly here to worship with us every weekend. There's a reason people drive here every week. A church alive is worth the drive! Life is too short to belong to a dead church. I've preached in many of them. I can preach one sermon in a dead church and it immediately becomes two sermons; my first one and my last one. I want to go where God and God's people are. I want to preach to folks that are hungry, not people that sit there like a bump on a bullfrog weakly whimpering, *"feed me, feed me, feed me."* I want to go where the people are hungry for the things of God. I want to go somewhere that I can open the Bible and say, "the Bible says... the Bible says... the Bible says!" ...and it stirs people's homes, and it stirs people's hearts, and it does something in their life, and it makes them want to walk out and turn the world upside down for the Kingdom of Jesus. That's the kind of church I want to be involved in.

Resurrection Power

And he said unto me, Son of man, can these bones live? And I answered, O Lord God, thou knowest.

~ Ezekiel 37:3

In verse three Ezekiel tells us that God is like, *let me ask you a question Ezekiel, can these bones be resurrected? Can breath and bodies be placed upon these dry bones in the valley? "Can these bones live?"* What a good question. So I ask you Church, can these bones live? Can a dry dead church spring up in revival? Do you believe that God can still revive this Great nation in the name of Jesus? I wouldn't have written this book if I didn't believe it.

Do you still believe that God can send a global revival? Do you still believe that Jesus is the only way to heaven? Do you still believe the Bible is the Word of God? Do you still believe the Holy Spirit is still alive and active and real and vibrant and working in our hearts? Do we believe that these bones can live? Yes, we believe these bones can live! Yes, we believe that God can send revival. I'm convinced He has already begun.

Son of Man

Let me emphasize something in this text that I don't want you to miss. The Lord put this on me when I was praying at the tree. In verse three we read, "And he said to me, Son of man..." Notice that he didn't say Son of God or Son of thunder. He said, "Son of man." Do you know why? Because God often reminds us in the context of His Scripture that it is the regular, normal, ordinary people that he uses for His glory. There wasn't one special thing about Ezekiel. As a matter of fact, if you think I get halfcocked and crazy sometimes, Ezekiel leaves me in the dust. On one occasion, he plum stripped his clothes off, laid on his side, and preached buck naked in the middle of the road. And when only half the crowd got right with God, he laid on his other side and continued to preach buck naked until the other half got mad or got born again.

I've never been one to start shucking off my clothes on a Sunday morning, Praise God. This guy was crazy! And people look at me and say, *"man, y'all have made some crazy decisions."* And I say, "Not THAT crazy. That's beyond Middle Tennessee hillbilly redneck crazy right there." But I get struck every time by the fact that over and over God called Ezekiel the "Son of man." It's a recurring phrase to remind us that the prophets were just as much human as we are. "Son of man" is also the name Jesus most often called Himself, partly to diffuse His enemies, I believe, but also to remind us of His absolute identification with us as a man, fully human, though still fully God. But unlike Jesus, Ezekiel was fully human. He was a down to earth, uneducated man. God didn't use him based on his qualifications. He called him and gave him the qualifications. I'm glad to know you also can be used by God if you really want it. He can do something in your life if you want Him to do something in your life. The only person keeping you from that is you. That's all.

12

God Wants You

God has been looking for you for a long time. You say, "my life's a mess." God's been looking for a mess like you for days, weeks, and years. He said, "I sought for a man among them that should make up the hedge and stand in the gap and I found none." (Ezekiel 22:30).

May God soon say He found one... He found two... He found 100... He found FIVE HUNDRED among those who read this book! May we get so filled with the glory of God that we spill out on other people just by accident, and just by proximity they get blessed for being around us.

Ezekiel received it then, and by the power of God he's sharing it with us now. Any simple, natural, ordinary man or woman can be used by God to turn a nation around. I believe God just wants to use ordinary people today just as He did in the days of the Bible. Age won't matter, gender won't matter, and race absolutely won't matter. God wants you no matter what you've done in the past. He loves to use the weak things of the world to confound the mighty, the dirt-poor things of the world to confound the rich, and the ignorant uneducated of the world to confound the wise. God has tarried this long so that more could find Him.

God doesn't need a single one of us, but He wants all of us to serve Him willfully and commune with Him as His children. "Son of man." I see why Jesus loved that name. Don't ever think that you have to be more than what you are or that you have to have more than what you have. God is ready to use you right where you are. Once you commit, your life will be changed forever.

Everything You Need

God made you in His image for His glory. When God looked at Moses, He didn't say," I need to give you this, I need to give you that, and I need to give you the other thing." He asked, "what do you have in your hand?" Moses answered, "a stick." And God said, "then you have more than enough to work with."

He didn't give Moses something else, He used what Moses already had. Yet everybody's like, "Well, I'd serve God if I had more money." No, you wouldn't. If you won't serve God broke, you surely won't serve God when you've got money in your pocket.

"Well, if I had more time, if my situation would turn around, if my kids weren't so crazy, I'd served the Lord." I enjoy serving the Lord *with* my crazy kids! I believe the Lord wants to use some of you in far more powerful ways than you think. And some of you already know your call but are waiting for something. You've got to realize that it's unlikely that He's going to give it to you until you start to boldly use the voice He already gave you. He's waiting for you use it to impact the sphere of influence He already gave you, all for His glory and the betterment of the Kingdom, whether it's 2 people or thousands. In other words, stop making excuses and just let God use you! "Son of man." It's amazing what you can get out of one short phrase in the Bible.

Speak!

Again he said unto me, Prophesy upon these bones, and say unto them, O ye dry bones, hear the word of the Lord.

~ Ezekiel 37:4

"Can these bones live? And I answered, "Oh, Lord God, thou knowest." Ezekiel was like, "I don't have the foggiest, but You do." I have no idea. They're dry. They're dead. There are many of them. Then in verse four we see, "Again, he said unto me, prophesy upon these bones..." How beautiful is that? There were no living people in the valley at this point. There were just bones. That's it. A graveyard. God didn't say, "gather the crowd under the tent and prophesy to the people." Nope. He said, "prophesy to the bones." Speak to the death. Speak to the demonic. Speak, speak, speak to the bones that they may live!

Sometimes we're trying to speak to things that God never called us to speak to. Sometimes we're trying to do something that God never called us to do or to be something that God never called us to be. He said, "do you see the bones?" Yeah. "Can they live?" I don't know. "Well, let's find out together... speak to the bones! Speak to the death!"

Speaking to the Problems

I am convinced that the reason people are hungry for churches like ours is because we're speaking directly to the biggest problems. We're prophesying to the bones. We're not just sitting around giving self-help talks and motivational guru speeches and telling everybody that every day is a Friday, or that your bills are always going to be paid, or that it's always going to be sunny, or that you'll never have a headache, your dog will always love you, your wife will never be mad at you, your kids will always obey you, you're going to live in a mansion, and things are going to be oh so good and hunky and dory and glorious. If you read the Bible and follow Jesus, it may not turn out so hot for you in these days.
"Yea, all that live Godly in Christ Jesus shall suffer persecution." (2 Timothy 3:12)

Persecution is coming. Let's speak to the bones. You're not reading this book because you saw a few videos with some soft spoken little guy on YouTube or on Twitter or on Facebook or on TikTok that said, *"now, dearly beloved, the Bible tells us that we must be loving and sooo compassionate to this wicked and godless culture... I apologize if I've ever said anything whatsoever to even remotely hurt your feelings... If I have, we will make sure that we set up an extra special section of the tent to serve as a safe space for your feelings... Please come and visit us any Sunday that you wish, and if you don't wish, we love you anyhow."*

      I wouldn't come to hear myself if I preached anything like that. You're reading this book because we're calling it what it is. We're calling out the wickedness. We're calling out the crooked politicians. We're calling it murder when they kill babies. We're saying it's wrong. We're saying it's lawless. We're saying it's an affront to God Almighty, and for that we're saying we ought to put an end to it forever. We believe in traditional marriage. If it goes against God and the absolute freedom He gifted us in this amazing nation, we're calling it out for what it is, and I believe that's why you're reading this now. You're not looking for me to soften the message. You're reading this book because we're trying to resurrect the bones by speaking to the bones in every way the Lord allows. I'm preaching to the needs of the hour, and the needs of the hour are for real boldness in these last days.

Standing on the Word

It's also important to see that God didn't tell Ezekiel to preach to the crowd, He said to preach to the bones before the crowd shows up. "Prophesy upon these bones, and say unto them, O ye dry bones, hear the word of the Lord." God isn't going to use a bag full of gimmicks to resurrect the bones. The only gimmick we have at our church is the word of God. I have nothing else to stand on, literally, as the Word of God is right here in the floor to remind me what I stand on. We have a Bible displayed under glass just behind the pulpit, and it's opened up to Isaiah 61:1 that reads:

"The Spirit of the Lord God is upon me; because the Lord hath anointed me to preach good tidings unto the meek; he hath sent me to bind up the brokenhearted, to proclaim liberty to the captives, and the opening of the prison to them that are bound"

~ Isaiah 61:1

That's no gimmick. That's the word of God, and I mean every word of it every time I speak it or read it. There is one thing that I am convinced the Lord will bless—His word. We don't have to coin clever new catch phrases. You know why I never have to worry if God is going to do what God has promised? Because the Bible has its own built-in power source.

On that morning at the tree, I wasn't like, "Oh my goodness, Lord, Ezekiel chapter 37... that's such a daunting passage of scripture... it's so prophetically spooky... please, Lord, don't make me... let me preach on something that I've got memorized... let me quote some verses that I have said a thousand times… let me preach a contemporary message that makes everyone feel warm and fuzzy." Do you know why I'm not worried about it? Because all I have to do is get up and read the Bible and it preaches itself!

A Message to Your Pastors

I've heard many pastors say in effect, "You know, it takes me like, five hours to get ready for a 30-minute sermon." I'm all for preparation. Really, I am. Even though some folks might hear me once and disagree, I'm all for preparation. But seriously, the stories in the Bible don't change, so I don't get it. I'm like, okay, you took five hours to study what? And I'll get something like, "You know, I want to tell people about the deeper points of Zacchaeus." What in the world? That little dude has been stuck in a tree for 2000 years and the story hasn't changed one bit! And the woman at the well has always been at the well. She's not suddenly in a coffee shop. And Bartimaeus has always been blind up to the point Jesus touched him! "Well, I've gotta make sure I get it right." Pastors, Lazarus was dead for four days, and the story hasn't changed one bit! Too many of us are trying to impress people with our eloquence or clever spin when all we have to do is impact people with the bold truth of what the Word of God already says. Just open the Word and let it preach. The Lord said you'd better preach to these bones! Ezekiel just showed up and preached to the bones as the Holy Spirit directed. There's not a whole lot of preparation needed to do that; just obedience.

The Other Samson and Elijah

When I first started preaching, I didn't have anybody to preach to, so I preached to two goats in a barn. Thank God I practiced with them because it prepared me for all goats I've met in the ministry, there's no doubt about it. But I'm not joking. They were named Samson and Elijah. I figured I might as well preach to them since anything with horns on its head could be of the devil and probably needs some Gospel, right? It can't hurt. So, I didn't have a crowd, I didn't have social media, and there wasn't a YouTube, thank God. I just locked myself in a barn at 212 Woodcraft Rd. in Murfreesboro, Tennessee, which is the address of the Good Shepherd Children's Home where I was saved as a teen. When I practiced, I would chain the door plumb closed. I didn't want any of the others to see me acting crazy.

If you can believe it, I'd put on a suit and tie in a barn, kicking up manure and sawdust, jumping around and swinging from the rafters, acting like Billy Sunday. I was just preaching my heart out to those goats. You might ask, "do you think they liked it?" Well, every time I got done, they'd say, "A-a-a-a-men brother Greg!" So I believe they liked it, praise God. And if they didn't, I'm my own favorite preacher, so it was always a good time! I literally started out by preaching to goats. I wasn't preaching to crowds. And I certainly wasn't preaching to millions of people around the world on Facebook. Sometimes you just have to walk it out the way God tells you to walk it out, even when you can't see what God is doing in your life. Can these bones live? Preach to them and see!

Through God Alone

"Thus saith the Lord God unto these bones; Behold, I will cause breath to enter into you, and ye shall live"
~ Ezekiel 37:5

Notice in verse five the Lord says, I will cause breath to enter into you, and you shall live. That's revival. Don't miss that it's God saying it and it's God sending it. Even if we could resurrect Billy Graham to preach the word of God in every church and get him to sign everyone's Bible, if God doesn't send it, it's not coming no matter who is preaching. We don't get revival from a man. We don't get revival from a network. We don't get revival from some denominational hierarchy. We get revival because God breathes life into a dead church. That's the only way we get revival.

And I will lay sinews upon you, and will bring up flesh upon you, and cover you with skin, and put breath in you, and ye shall live; and ye shall know that I am the Lord.
~ Ezekiel 37:6

Here's the beautiful thing about this epic passage and so many others in the Bible that speak to the subject of revival and awakening: You can always find the validity of a move of God when God alone gets the glory. Notice Ezekiel didn't get the glory. The bones didn't get the glory. No, this was done by the Lord. It was an obvious move of God then, just as it will take an obvious move of God now.

Remember what happened when Elijah called fire down from heaven? For twelve hours the prophets of Baal cried out to a false God and the Bible says that there was no answer. Do you know why? Because there was no Baal. Not then and not now. After the prophets of Baal failed, Elijah stood up and repaired the altar. Why? Because there will always be some repair and restoration before revival comes. So he rebuilt the altar and he prayed fifty-four words. Not fifty-four days, not fifty-four minutes, not fifty-four verses, but fifty-four words that comprise a single verse in the Bible. The fire of God fell so gloriously that it licked up the altar and the sacrifice. The fire consumed it all, and it melted the hearts of the people.

Do you remember the people's response? They fell on their knees and said, "the Lord, He is the God... the Lord, He is the God... the Lord, He is the God!" They didn't say, "rah rah, bish boom bah, three cheers for Elijah, that's the best preaching we've ever heard in our life!" No. When real revival comes, God will get all the glory for it. We can't rob Him of a single ounce of His glory.

13

Behold a Shaking

So I prophesied as I was commanded: and as I prophesied, there was a noise, and behold a shaking, and the bones came together, bone to his bone.

~ Ezekiel 37:7

Elijah called out to the bones. God asked, "Can the bones live?" Ezekiel likely thought, I don't know, but let's try it together... bones come alive in the name of God! Verse seven says that there was "a noise." In our culture right now there's a lot of noise. There's a lot of chaos. But "God is not the author of confusion" (1 Corinthians 14:33).

Americans are addicted to noise. Church people are addicted to noise. We're addicted to music, we're addicted to newscasts, we're addicted to TikTok and YouTube videos. It's when things get quiet that we get nervous, because in the midst of the noise we have to get silent before God. That's when the still small voice begins to speak to us and makes us uncomfortable, which is a good place to be. The Bible says that after this noise was heard, there was a shaking. And the shaking—not the noise—is what brought the bones together. Until we are willing to experience the shaking and the shakedown, God is not going to bring life to the bones and bring us back together as a mighty army for His glory. These things must happen.

My Shaking, My Breaking

In Revelation Chapter 3, the Bible says, "I counsel thee to buy of me gold tried in the fire, that thou mayest be rich." Do you know what that means in context? It means that when a church suffers together, it brings them closer. When God shakes out some things and shakes out some people and shakes brokenness to the surface, He's doing it for the purpose of blessing us, but first He breaks us. If there is no shaking, there is no awakening from the Holy Spirit.

About three years ago, when I went through the darkest storms of my life, I never thought that our church would be experiencing what we're seeing right now. I thought my storms would leave a permanent mark against my life and my character. The media soiled the beauty of our church body even though they should only have come after me, if anyone at all. We were growing by leaps and bounds in those days, but it was the wrong kind of growth. It was Greg growth, not God growth.

We had a lot of people here that idolized my preaching, I know that now, but I was too swept up in it all to see it. Back then, the church was a place where my fiery style had become the primary attraction, not the Lord, and God has a way of breaking that nonsense out of peoples' hearts. I don't want to lose track of the message by going into the whole painful story in this book, but I do want you to know that God has since brought a great number of families back. Many of them left because they were heartbroken during the time and didn't know what to believe, and I truly get it, but we'll never go back that way again.

I've seldom addressed those days in a public forum, because when it's all said and done, to God be the glory for the shaking and the breaking. What He's done is His work and His road to restoration for me, and it has been more beautiful than anything I could have ever imagined. All that said, I would not have wished my shaking and my breaking on my worst enemy, but

I wouldn't change a second of it because it has defined who I am today, and it has changed everything about our church.

A Real Move of God

At the peak of the shaking I felt like a rag doll. The Lord just shook it all right out of me. As I watched a mass exodus from our church, I felt like there was no more life, no more breath, and no more fight left in me. To put that into perspective, the amount of people that walked away from our church in those days is equal to the amount of people gathering under our tent at the time of this book, somewhere between 500 and 750. That was a daunting number of people to lose from the family. But again, God began to bring people back and began to bring new people in, and now folks are flying and driving in from all over the place.

I say all that to say this. Since those days, our church has been praying for a REAL move of God... for a genuine revival, for a real outpouring of the Holy Spirit, and I know we weren't alone. I believe God heard from heaven and said, "Oh, I've got that coming... but I have something I need to do first... I have some more shaking that needs to happen." And God shook us good and broke us of things only He could break.

In a "beauty from ashes" God-like way, in our weakness, He strengthened us. In our brokenness, He healed us. First He humbled me, then He emboldened me in a different way. He gave me a voice that I never really had before, and the very thing that I thought would destroy me became the foundation from which God has been able to help and bless so many. He turned my pain and my healing into our platform—the plow we've put our hands to in this season—and we're not looking back.

Preach to the Wind

The Word of God said there was a great shaking, and the bones came together. Then Ezekiel said:

And when I beheld, lo, the sinews and the flesh came up upon them, and the skin covered them above: but there was no breath in them. Then said he unto me, Prophesy unto the wind, prophesy, son of man, and say to the wind, Thus saith the Lord God; Come from the four winds, O breath, and breathe upon these slain, that they may live.

~ Ezekiel 37:8-9

Notice that bodies formed from mere bones, but they still had no breath. And that's where we are in the American Church. A lot of bodies but no breath. A lot of bodies but no life. In verse nine we read, "Then said he unto me, Prophesy unto the wind..." I love that. First, He said to preach to the bones and then He said to preach to the wind. If I walked out into a windstorm and began to preach to the wind, you would think I had lost my ever-loving mind, and rightly so. Ezekiel was told by God to go scream at the wind. Can you imagine? "Hello wind... hello four corners of the wind... north, south, east and west." He literally preached to the wind!

Why does God say to preach to the bones and preach to the wind? Because if we're not careful, we might forget a beautiful principle. We walk in the very authority of God and need to share His supernatural power with boldness. We don't walk in that authority because we're ashamed of it! And in the name of God, the bones and the wind are always subject to Jesus. Preach to the wind!

The Calmest Boy Ever

The other night when I was in Somerset, Kentucky I met a family that had eleven children. Six of them were foster children, and I sincerely admired everything I learned about them. One of their boys who looked to be about 12 years old was sitting on a picnic blanket (it was an outdoor event) and while I was shaking hands with all the family and hugging them and praying with them and taking pictures, this little boy calmly sat there playing with an action figure. And I thought, man, he's the most chill little dude I've ever met. He was just calmly sitting there having a good time and he was as respectful and kind as a boy can be. When I commented about him, his daddy told me this amazing story:

He's the child we actually wanted you to meet at this revival, and that's why we're here." He continued, "about six months ago, we couldn't control this kid. He would scream every moment of the day, with blood curdling screams. He would pull out his own hair, and if you got too close, he would pull your hair too. He would even spit on you and slap at you and smash things if you let him. We got so exhausted with it that one day our pastor preached on praying over folks. We've never even thought about it, but there he was in the middle of church screaming and climbing the walls and pulling my hair. I just held his arms down, picked him up, and carried him to the altar. When we got down to the altar people at our church thought we were crazy. But we prayed over him in the name of Jesus, and we claimed the power of Jesus and the blood of Jesus. We just called it for what it was.

Then he stood back and his eyes bugged out of his head like two Jimmy Dean sausage patties as he said, "I'm gonna tell you preacher, that's the last time we had an episode like that." If you have trouble believing this man's story, then you're reading the wrong book, and you haven't been reading the Bible. I believe in the power of God. I believe that the name of Jesus and the blood of Jesus still have immeasurable power. I believe that greater is He that is in you than he that is in the world, and that we can still have authority in Jesus' name! God promises all of this and more. Ezekiel preached to the wind and he preached to the bones and the wind and the bones did what he said, because he walked in the authority that God gave him. Oh breath, breathe upon the slain that they may live! Do you have this faith? If not, don't you want it?

So I prophesied as he commanded me, and the breath came into them, and they lived, and stood up upon their feet, an exceeding great army.

~ *Ezekiel 37:10*

Ezekiel said, "So I prophesied as he commanded me..." Even when it looked foolish, even when his heart was broken, even when it seemed like nobody was listening, even when it seemed like nothing was happening, he did what God told him to do. Obedience will be the most difficult choice you will ever make. Ezekiel prophesied as he was commanded by God, and the breath came into the bones, and they lived, stood up upon their feet, and formed an exceeding great army.

No longer casual, calm, lukewarm, lazy, or lackadaisical— these resurrected men stood upon their feet with bodies and breath and a powerful calling from God. The prophetic word that came to them caused them to stand with a wrought-iron backbone. And they weren't just standing meek and mild. They were an exceedingly great army that was ready to go to war!

The Weapons of Our Warfare

When we speak of war, we're speaking of the war between good and evil, and that is best fought in the spiritual realm. So let's be reminded that our weapons are spiritual, not of man. As recorded in the Foreword to this book, the Apostle Paul tells us, "We wrestle not against flesh and blood, but against principalities and powers and spiritual wickedness in high places." (Ephesians 6:12)

The Bible also tells us, *"For the weapons of our warfare are not carnal, but mighty through God to the pulling down of strongholds. Casting down imaginations, and every high thing that exalteth itself against the knowledge of God, and bringing into captivity every thought to the obedience of Christ;"* (2 Corinthians 10:4-5), and it also exhorts us to *"Put on the whole armour of God, that ye may be able to stand against the wiles of the devil"* (Ephesians 6:11), and always to *"stand in these evil wicked days of deception."* (Ephesians 6:13) Refer back to the Foreword on page 1 for the Apostle Paul's full inventory of our spiritual armor.

The church is under a spell of deception in America. The longer I preach, the more tears I shed. People see me as they will in short snippets, but they don't know my heart. They don't know how this church has labored and fasted and prayed for all we're starting to see unfold. But when I read Ezekiel 37 on that morning under my prayer tree, it deeply convicted me. "They stood up an exceeding great army." So please hear me Church and hear me well. I mince not my words, nor do I apologize for what's about to fall from my lips.

We must shift our focus into the realm of spiritual warfare and walk it out on earth as it is in heaven. We must know the real enemy and recognize that the culture is not only against the Church but is buck wild psychotic against God Himself, and Jesus by name. From henceforth and forevermore in these days of wickedness, I proclaim before God that I want to be a leader of a spiritual army, and God is indeed raising up an army! When they attack the Bible and when they attack the Church, we'll live by one phrase. THIS MEANS WAR. So let's armor up as the Lord instructed. It's high time that we rise up with the breath of God in us as the exceedingly great army that He prophesied in His Word!

Closing Prayer

As I close Part III, please say this prayer with me. Thank You
Father in heaven for the power of the Holy Spirit. Thank you for
the authority of the word of God…forgive us for not walking in it
Lord. Right this moment we stand in the victory that we have. Not
a victory we're fighting *for*, but a victory we are fighting *from*. For
we are already victors in Christ. We know how it all pans out in
the end. Your word does not say "oh me" it says "Amen," so let it
be. Even so, come Lord Jesus. God, give us a burden for the dry
cold dustiness of fake, dead, hypocritical, lukewarm Christianity in
the American Church. Lord, we know that the persecution is here,
and we know that it's going to intensify, but I am convinced it is
going to thin out the ranks and raise up an army of people that
realize that real revival comes when God's people push back
against the tidal wave of persecution, in spirit and truth, in word
and action. We know the Gospel is hated and that the name of
Jesus is maligned and that the Bible is spat upon in these days, but
we stand. We will live for You, and we proclaim that we will die
for You. So God, work today as only You can, here where I am
and everywhere around the world. We hear Your call to fight for
what we know is right. So Father bless what we have read in this
book and, even more, bless how we will apply it to our hearts, in
Jesus' name, amen.

Part IV: Proclamation

Fear them not therefore: for there is nothing covered, that shall not be revealed; and hid, that shall not be known. What I tell you in darkness, that speak ye in light: and what ye hear in the ear, that preach ye upon the housetops. And fear not them which kill the body, but are not able to kill the soul: but rather fear him which is able to destroy both soul and body in hell. Are not two sparrows sold for a farthing? and one of them shall not fall on the ground without your Father. But the very hairs of your head are all numbered. Fear ye not therefore, ye are of more value than many sparrows. Whosoever therefore shall confess me before men, him will I confess also before my Father which is in heaven. But whosoever shall deny me before men, him will I also deny before my Father which is in heaven. Think not that I am come to send peace on earth: I came not to send peace, but a sword." ~ Jesus

MATTHEW 10:26-34

14

Speak Now or Forever Hold Your Peace

There's a passage that's been on my heart for much of 2020 and I've long known it would become a central theme of this book. I have to admit that maybe my personal fears and insecurities have given me pause before applying this passage to the here and now. But I believe it speaks directly to where we are all living as the Church, not just our local church, but the big-C Church—the body of Christ in America, in the culture, and around the world.

We're going to take another look into the life and Scripture of the prophet Ezekiel from the Old Testament, and I'm going to share my heart with you a bit, and just chit chat with you a little while longer as we approach the end of this book. I also want to open up some topics that I'm working through and living through as a Christian and a pastor that we the Church are all walking through together.

Whether you live across the street from us at Global Vision or across the state of Tennessee or live many states away or even somewhere else around the globe, I want you to know that we consider all of you to be part of the family. It doesn't matter if you've only visited us one time or never before, if you're a believer you're part of the family. I'm grateful you've found your way to this book and hope you've found the opportunity to hear the Gospel as we preach it every week live and streaming online all week long, especially if you don't currently have a church you can attend live and in person. Our online sermons carry the same Biblical truth, transparent honesty, and Holy Spirit guidance found in this book plus all the passion you'd expect from a revival tent packed with worshippers. Nothing beats a live gathering, but at least you can still get the living word online, for now.

Opening Prayer

As we dive into Part 4, please speak this prayer with me. Father, I know there are people reading this book for 100 different reasons. But at the end of the day, we're reading because we want to hear from You, and we want to worship You in spirit and in truth. And Lord, I know all is vain unless the Spirit of the Holy One comes down, so I pray that you would make this message about Jesus, and that you'd make this book about the authority of the Bible, the power of the Holy Spirit, and your love and forgiveness, Father. So Lord, give us boldness, give us courage, give us biblical soundness, and give all readers of this book the ears to hear what You say through all we read. We're going to be careful to give you the honor and glory and praise due your glorious name Jesus, so it is in your name we pray, amen.

The Lord Speaks in Mysterious Ways

As I shared in Part 1, when I first began to speak about my "blue flame" dream during our live services, I also talked about all the confirmations that have been pouring in. Suddenly there was a deluge of folks who felt the Lord wanted them to share what He had put on their hearts. Whether they reached me by phone, or by approaching me at a revival meeting, or by flying into Tennessee for a single Wednesday night service, each dropped the same nugget of truth in our spirit, and in each case these confirmations were virtually verbatim. In unprecedented fashion, I was hearing the exact same message that someone else had already told us, and that someone else had already written to us, and that someone else had already called to tell us. These confirmations continue to this day.

As the Lord first began to show up through these people with such startling alignment, I remained careful to whom and to what degree I shared the details of this unified message. I want everything that I do to be to the glory of God, through the power of the Holy Spirit, and nothing more. I want to honor and exalt the Gospel of the Lord Jesus Christ, and I want to know it's always the Spirit of God talking, not the people.

At one point we had a meeting scheduled for nearly a month with folks who originally reached out to me on Twitter, and I almost had to reschedule it, but something compelled me to make it happen as originally scheduled. So they flew in from Colorado Springs for a single sit down meeting at Olive Garden, and I made sure not to say Jack Spratt about any of the confirmations my wife and I had been receiving during the preceding months before first hearing what they had to say. Lo and behold, once they shared what they came to share, I got emotional. I can get emotional every now and then, but not often over spaghetti, and there I was getting choked up just thinking about the fact that God sent two more people to tell us things they had no way of knowing unless the Spirit revealed it to them. Issues no one knew we had been praying about. Nobody else knew the context of any of these things, yet they were able to speak them plainly, as if they were just reading it off a page.

When the spirit of God is moving through people and telling them to speak into you—as long as it doesn't contradict the truth and the authority of this book—I've come to a place where I'm going to receive it and stand on it. So there we were, in Olive Garden, at Providence Mall in Mount Juliet, small town USA, and I cried like a baby. I couldn't stop thinking, "God is doing what God has always promised that He was going to do and He's doing it right here." He's opening doors we could never imagine, and He used this overwhelming outpouring of encouragement and confirmation to ensure I closed this book with another message God wrote to us through Ezekiel more than 2500 years ago.

Getting in God's Way

In 1 Corinthians 15 Paul said that we ought to pray for God to open doors that no man can shut and to shut doors that no man can open. By now you might have already figured this out about me and our people at Global Vision… if God opens a door, we're going to run through it. If God shuts a door, we aren't kicking it in and we aren't knocking on it in effort to get back in. We're just going to turn around and start going in the other direction. I want to be like the servant of Abraham who said, "I being in the way, the Lord led me." (Genesis 24:27)

I just want to get in God's way where he wants me to be. I just want God to lead us and guide us, and I know He's going to do that through the context of His word no matter how many saints He sends to alert us. In Ezekiel 33 there is an urgent message to the church of Jesus Christ in the United States of America, and it applies directly to where we are today. If you can't see that we are in desperate need of revival, you couldn't have read the previous three sections of this book. These are those days, and it's time.

I'm not just saying this because churches are closing down, some permanently. And I'm not just saying this because of the mandates and darkness we covered in the first three parts of this book. I'm talking about the tragic reality that the church in America isn't just shrinking into silence, it has actually fallen fast asleep. We are watching Biblical prophecy being fulfilled in context every single week before our very eyes, and it's almost like churches are just sitting there numb, and pastors are just standing there in a daze, and no one is catching the vision or getting excited about what they're seeing unfold. Most everybody is discouraged about the violence in the news, but I'm actually encouraged, because God said it was going to have to happen.

We already know that in the last days, extreme wickedness and evil would come, and that men will be lovers of themselves (2 Timothy 3:2). No matter how you slice it, these are those days, so I don't get discouraged. I'm not going to walk around with my lip dragging the ground or be like, "Oh my goodness, I've got to go to church again... I can't believe I've got to get up and grab that microphone and go under that hot tent to preach again." I can hardly wait to gather with the people of God... I wish we had church at six o'clock in the morning!

They Prayed for These Days

We're watching the Bible being fulfilled in ways that those who came before us could only dream of, literally, so I can hardly sit still. The generation that we're living in is the very generation that the New Testament Church has always prayed would be theirs but wasn't. They prayed for what we're being given. They also prayed for spiritual persecution to come against the church, because they knew the church never grows in comfort and only truly grows in persecution and affliction. We are living in days that the Apostle Paul could only dream of. We are living in days that Matthew, Mark, Luke, and John could only hope for. These saints prayed for the return of the Lord and the coming of His Kingdom... soon. Though Jesus said they wouldn't see it, he confirmed there was a generation that would see it all come to pass. Imagine how every generation since has prayed He was talking about them. Now here we are.

We're living in a generation where in just six months we have leapt 50 years in the prophetic timeline of the Bible, and I think it's just getting geared up. I think it's just now starting. But if you can't see it, it's because you don't want to see it. It's because you refuse to see it. And the Church is walking around with blinders on not paying attention to the truth of the Word of God because what God said was going to happen is finally happening right before our eyes.

Speak Now...

Being a pastor, it's an occupational hazard for me to have a lot of different ceremonies to officiate. Funerals and weddings, for example. Of all the weddings that I have performed or been part of, there is something that the old-time preachers used to say that I think is sorely missing these days. It's rarely ever said in modern church weddings—and probably for good reason. But you old timers (I say that respectfully) will remember when the preacher would be all suited and booted like a third person on a wedding cake, and the bride and the groom would nervously stand in front of a house full of folks who were also all dressed up. And they would go through all the "I dos" and all the "I don'ts," and the vows, and the kissing, and the exchanging of rings, and throwing birdseed at people, and all of those fun things.

Then there was that one not-so-fun thing that always had everyone holding their breath, especially the bride and groom. Before the pastor or officiant would say "I now pronounce you husband and wife," and Mr. and Mrs. So-and-So performed their big wet sloppy kiss in front of everybody (and embarrassed themselves forevermore on camera), the old time preachers would say, "if there's anybody up in the house that has a just cause for this couple not to come together (again, there's probably a very good reason we don't ask that these days), if there's any reason that these two should not be divinely brought together in holy matrimony... speak now, or forever hold your peace." They'd be like, "*look, if you're gonna say it, you'd better say it right now before we hitch these two together. If you're ever gonna put it out there, you'd better do it right now. If you're ever gonna spill the beans you'd better kick the bucket over right here and right now.*" Speak now, or forever hold your peace.

History Repeats Itself

I believe that God Almighty is saying this right now to the church in the United States and around the world. If you're going to speak, you'd better speak now. If you're going to preach, you'd better preach now. If you're going to pray, you'd better pray now. If you're going to fast, you'd better fast now. If you're going to believe God for miracles, you'd better believe God for miracles now. Speak now, or forever hold your peace, Church!

When discussing speaking out, I often hear people say things like, "Well, you know, if I was alive back in the days of Nazi Germany, I believe I would have said something... I believe I would have made a phone call... I believe I would have turned them in, I would have stood up to it, I would have stood out, I would have..."

What would you have done? Before you answer, let me tell you the truth. Whatever you think you would have been doing then, is exactly what you aren't doing right now. Or we can put it this way. If you aren't doing it now, you wouldn't have done it then. It's easy to talk about what we would have done a long time ago in a situation we'll never have to face. *"Well, I'll tell you one thing, I would have stood up against Hitler, that's for sure... I would have spoken out, I would have done all I can to save the Jews, and I would have been bold in my faith!"* If that's true of you, why aren't you bold in your faith right now? The very things you say you would have done back then are the same things you aren't doing right now. Very few Jewish Holocaust era Christians spoke out. Ever. So, if you claim you'd stand with God to stop the Holocaust today, you'd better start speaking now or forever hold your peace.

15

The Battle at Hand

This year alone they're going to butcher millions of babies all the way up to their scheduled birthday when they're fully grown infants. I haven't heard a lot of Christians speaking out or trying to rescue them. I don't know about you, but I hear the Lord saying that we'd better speak now or forever hold our peace. I'm not afraid to get political over matters of faith, but how did abortion ever become a political issue? Abortion is murder no matter the age of the baby, but late term abortions are unconscionable. Tearing full grown babies to pieces in the womb is about as evil as it gets. How did we ever allow it to become legal and stay that way on our watch?

Ending abortion is an act of our faith, commanded by God, and I'll do whatever it takes to ensure you know we're one election away from losing the privilege to practice our faith and boldly speak out as we can right now. Truly, we're just one election away from losing our rights to speak out against ANYTHING, and since you're reading this book, I'm confident you know that. We've got to pay better attention to what is going on around us. We have got to read the Bible. We've got to get out of Facebook and get our faces in the good Book. If we don't realize what is upon us, we'll soon be getting arrested and sent to jail just for speaking out for the righteousness of Jesus Christ. It's already commonplace around the world, and to the globalists who are trying to label Christianity as hate speech the American church is the only thing standing in their way.

If the Church doesn't rise up to put people in the White House who defend our faith and defend babies in the womb, great persecution is at hand. GREAT persecution. So you'd better speak now or forever hold your peace. Eventually we're going to get the wrong person in there, great persecution is going to come, and I'm going to go to jail. Some of you are going to have to take up an offering to get me out, and most of you are going to live in regret that you didn't really speak out when you had the chance.

Speaking with Your Vote

If, like me, you'd rather delay the coming of those darkest days, and get one more chance to end abortion and bring justice to all the oppressed and share the Gospel with more of your friends and family, you'd better speak now. If we fail, it's not going to get any better. My Bible said it's going to get far worse. Evil men and deceivers shall wax worse and worse, being deceived and deceiving others.

Churches are going to get permanently shut down, the government is going to go crazy on us, and the mobs in the streets are going to go buck wild. It seems like we're witnessing a dress rehearsal right now, doesn't it? We have to speak out now if we hope to buy more time. And if you think you don't have a voice, you're wrong. At very least you can speak with your vote. In fact, at this time, there is no louder way to speak than with your vote and your encouragement to other Christians to do the same. Vote the Bible now, or forever hold your peace.

There is no Back Door

It has always amazed me to see how many people slip out through the back door after the dust settles and try to act like they were heroic during the battle. Five years from now People will be saying to me, "Woo! man, I'm so glad I stood up and spoke out." The same people who didn't say Jack Sprat when we were going to jail will rewrite themselves onto the front lines, but the Lord won't forget who truly answered the call. If you can't stand for God when things are bad, don't think you can jump up and brag about standing for God when everything is good.

I'm going to speak out against butchering babies no matter how mad the baby killers get. I'm going to speak out about all this racial wickedness that we have going on in the United States and all of this politically motivated destruction and division that we're witnessing no matter how bad it gets. I'm going to speak out about churches closing their doors when 100% of them should be open no matter how things shake out. I'm going to speak now.

What I have to remember is that I don't have to stand before YOU at the judgment seat, I have to stand before God, and I'm not going to have the *Bible Baptistic Porky Pig syndrome* when God asks, "why didn't you tell them?" I'm not going to stutter and stumble to answer the Lord, because I'm going to tell them! I'm going to be able to say, "That's on them Lord! Please rewind that divine DVD and watch it Lord...You'll see that I said it. I told the people that it was going to get crazy evil, I warned them Lord!" So why are we who speak out in the minority? Because people are far too worried about the approval of man when they should be consumed with the approval of God.

Can it Be Delayed?

Again the word of the Lord came unto me, saying, Son of man, speak to the children of thy people, and say unto them, When I bring the sword upon a land, if the people of the land take a man of their coasts, and set him for their watchman...
~ *Ezekiel 33:1-2*

In this passage, notice verse one starts with "Again." The reason it says "again" is because God told Ezekiel the same thing earlier (recorded in chapter 3) that he was going to be a watchman to the nation of Israel. He said, "Again the word of the Lord came unto me, saying, Son of man, speak to the children of thy people, and say unto them, "When I bring the sword upon a land..."

Notice this is the judgment of God coming upon the land. The Bible says in 2 Peter that judgment must begin at the house of God. You might say, "I thought God was loving?" He is. "I thought God was forgiving?" He is. "I thought God was redemptive?" He is, but God is also holy, and because of His holiness, He's not going to overlook sin. Judgment may be delayed, but judgment is on its way. There is no doubt about that. That's a primary theme of the whole Bible... judgment may be delayed, but judgment will come.

The Lord said, warn them when I bring the sword upon the land. *"If the people of the land, take a man, take a man out their coasts, and set him for their watchman."* I'll get to the context and the application of what that means here in just a moment, but first let's look at the phrase in verse one where it says, "Again, the word of the Lord came unto me." Let's agree that there is no comparison between the word of a man and the word of the Lord.

The word of the Lord has a built-in power system. I don't have to fake it till I make it. I don't have to pretend. I don't have to show up, grab a microphone, jump on the stage and have a Jimmy Carter smile and just kind of get through it. I don't have to make anything up. I don't have to manufacture it. I don't have to preach it up or pray it down. The Word of God, the Gospel of Christ, "is the power of God unto salvation" (Romans 1:16). I don't have to fake it. So all I have to do is what Ezekiel and all the major prophets and all the minor prophets and all the Old Testament shepherds and all the New Testament apostles and prophets and evangelists and pastors and teachers did. All I have to do is preach what the Bible says.

The Sword of the Spirit

"The Bible says... the Bible says... the Bible says... the Bible says!" What I say doesn't matter unless the Bible says it, so you'd do well to pay attention to what it is saying to you right now. *"The grass withereth, the flower fadeth: but the word of our God shall stand for ever."* (Isaiah 40:8)

In the context of Ezekiel 33, He didn't say that the word of some preacher or the word of some seminary hierarchy, or the word of some denominational leader, or the word of Dr. Wigglejaw or Sister Bottlestopper. No, it says, "and the word of the Lord" came unto Him.

When you get a word from God, you'll be bold about it. When you get a word from God, you'll stand before kings or paupers and be bold about the truth that God has placed in your heart. Ephesians 6:17 refers to the Bible as "The sword of the Spirit." Not the envelope opener, not the butter knife, but "the sword."

For the word of God is quick, and powerful, and sharper than any twoedged sword, piercing even to the dividing asunder of soul and spirit, and of the joints and marrow, and is a discerner of the thoughts and intents of the heart.

~ Hebrews 4:12

Do you know why the Bible makes people nervous? Because it shows them who they are on the inside, not just on the outside. That's why we ought to be pitching a fit about what's going on in Portland and the other Democrat led cities embroiled in riots these days. Not only are they burning American flags but they're also burning Bibles in the streets, and the liberals and others on the left are okay with this Marxist evil. We've seen this Bible-burning trend in the recent past and 6 million innocent people lost their lives because no one spoke out for them. Yet most of us are just sitting around like a Billy goat eating briars or like a calf at a new gate thinking to ourselves, "well, that's the preacher's job to call that out." That's nonsense. I'm not the only one opening this book who is called to NOT be a coward. Every believer is commanded to be bold and courageous for the cause of the Gospel of Jesus Christ, if they truly believe.

Wandering from The Commandments

"The B-I-B-L-E, yes that's the book for me. I stand alone on the Word of God, the Word of God, the Word of God, the B-I-B-L-E." There's one thing I stand on, live on and will die by, and that's the truth of this book that we call the Bible. Jesus said in John 17:17, "Father sanctify them through thy truth: thy word is thy truth." That's the word I have hidden in my heart that I might not sin against God.

Wherewithal shall a young man cleanse his way? by taking heed thereto according to thy word. With my whole heart have I sought thee: O let me not wander from thy commandments.

~ Psalms 119:9-10

The American church has clearly wandered from the commandments. We've more than wandered. We've Ubered a long way out of God's direction. We've pulled a Jonah and God is about to swallow us up in the belly of a whale to get our attention. Meanwhile there's a modern-day Nineveh that needs someone to preach repentance.

Where are the Watch-Men?

Where Ezekiel 33 says, "when he seeth the sword come upon the land, if the people of the land take a man of their coast and set him for their watchman," the Lord isn't saying He's looking for a single watchman to answer this call. We clearly need people to stand up plurally and collectively to rise up, lift up a standard, and raise their voices in every corner of this nation, even in our neighborhoods. And I absolutely believe we need some watch-women too. Though women have basically carried the church for most of the last century, I believe women have an even greater role in the future of the local church.

In these last days, God is going to pour out His Spirit upon all flesh, not just the men. But just as I discussed in Part 1 concerning my blue flame dream, when the Spirit pours out in this way it will be the men that start getting right with God in startling ways, because we have a lot to start getting right. It's going to be the men that will repent. It's going to be the husbands, it's going to be the pastors, it's going to be the fathers. It's going to have to be the men who respond with greatest courage, and I hope to God it's not just the women who get fired up when they read that. Men, if you're getting nervous about what I'm saying, you're reading the wrong book. If that's you, wait ten more minutes and you're really going to be ticked off.

No Turning Back

I've come too far to turn back now. If you follow my short videos, you know I've already burned my long-time relationship with Dunkin' Donuts slap to the ground, so I've got very little left to lose, praise God. Seriously, we need to stop worrying about what we are going to lose while contending for our faith and fighting for justice and the rule of law in this land. We need some men to start acting like men. We need a few tents to fill up with testosterone. I'm telling you, some of you men need to go scream at a tree and get a deeper voice so you can stand up and use that voice for the glory of God. We need more men on these platforms rising up for the sake of Christianity in America.

When I see an invitation delivered in a church, if a hundred people come forward, eighty-nine of them will be women. That's inspiring to a degree, but I'm confused as to why so many men have abdicated their role and their responsibility in the local church. It appears all the cowardly men are just staying at home and not doing anything. Churches should be packed to overflow with men that are on fire for Jesus… men that want to do something meaningful for Jesus. But we have too many weak, lifeless men sending their wives and kids to church. These men need to get up and lead their families to the altar. God said we need a watchman, and in a world where a man's home is his castle, every man is being called up to duty—even if only to protect His own family from the persecution to come.

16

Blood on Our Hands?

If when he seeth the sword come upon the land, he blow the trumpet, and warn the people; Then whosoever heareth the sound of the trumpet, and taketh not warning; if the sword come, and take him away, his blood shall be upon his own head.

~ *Ezekiel 33:3-4*

Notice in this passage that Ezekiel can see the sword coming. He's paying attention to it. Please note that we're not looking for signs, we're simply depicting the seasons, and we're in a season right now that happens to be full of signs. Jesus told us in the Olivet Discourse, as recorded in Matthew 24, that we won't know the day or the hour of His return. We won't know the very moment, but as discussed in Part 1, Jesus ensured we would know what's going to happen to signal the end, and He warned us that we must pay attention to the season and be ready.

That fig tree Jesus talks about in Matthew 24:32 is getting heavy. It's about to sprout and the fruit is about to fall. In that context, the Bible says that Ezekiel sees what nobody else sees. He predicts what nobody else predicts. The Lord ensures he can see something coming so he can properly warn the people. "Then whosoever heareth the sound of the trumpet, and taketh not warning; if the sword come, and take him away, his blood shall be upon his own head." Let's get the mental picture here. The watchman would be set up at the wall and he had a set of stairs that he would climb up to to the top of the wall to see whatever might be approaching. His role is to guard the city.

Duties of the Watchman

Each one of the tribes and each one of the cities and each one of the communities would have watchmen to serve in this critical role, and many watchmen were needed to keep watch of their entire area of responsibility. Psalm 1:27 says that the watchman wakes in vain without the power of the Lord. They train him and teach him how to maintain the highest perspective while remaining vigilant. The watchmen have to pay very close attention and be greatly discerning while surveying the horizon. He has to know when the rain or a windstorm is coming, and he has to discern the difference between a small threat and an army that's coming to destroy the people of God.

The Lord tells Ezekiel to get up on the wall and keep watch, and He's telling us to do the same. Then when you see the enemy advancing, when you see the problem that you already discerned was coming, you'll blow the trumpet to warn your people. When the Bible references a trumpet, it's not talking about a modern brass instrument but the ceremonial ram's horn that we call a shofar. The watchmen would keep a large shofar with them at all times, and they would stand up on top of their section of the wall with this trumpet at the ready. When they would see the enemy advancing towards God's people, they would blow the trumpet with all their breath.

This is what Isaiah was referring to in Isaiah 58:1 when he said to lift up your voice like a trumpet... lift up your voice like a trumpet... lift up your voice like a trumpet and show my people their sins! He didn't say, *"Well, what I want you to do is get up in that tower, and when the enemy starts advancing, just look down at the people below and say in a soft and compassionate voice, 'ladies and gentlemen, you can believe this if you want to, it's up to you*

how you take this, because I'm just here to tell you something is
coming, but God forbid I get too stirred up.'"

"Too" Stirred Up?

Some people say to me, "Brother Locke, sometimes you just get
too angry." Please don't ever mistake my passion for anger. There's
a big difference. That said, when it comes to the watchmen of this
generation, I am indeed getting angry. I'm mad at the devil. And
I'm mad at lazy Christians who won't stand up and join me as I call
out the schemes of the devil. I know there are some points I could
frame a little better and curb my emotions a bit. I get it. But when
it's all said and done, I know God did not call me to silence, and
He did not call the preachers of this land to silence. Yet most are
living in abject silence, and this silence has become their surrender.
God has called us to boldly blow the trumpet and warn the people
that judgment is coming, that persecutions are coming, that the
enemy is advancing, and, in fact, that the enemy is already at the
gate.

As I write this, I've been trying to make a short TikTok
video for about three days, talking about the witchcraft and
Satanism that has crept into the church of the living God and
America. And I kid you not, there are definite forces trying to stop
me. I'm not one of these spooky kooky "look for the boogie man
under the bed" sort of people, but I'd bet you I've tried to shoot that
video 25 times to no avail. I tried to record it four or five times just
this morning. I'm usually pretty good at recording short videos like
this in one take. But every time I get on that phone to make this
particular video, somebody calls, or the phone turns off, or I
experience technical TikTok glitches, or somebody drives by and
honks their horn mid-stream, or something else crazy happens
before I can finish.

Here's my point for sharing this. The enemy can't stand it
when you expose him. And when you start exposing him, he starts
doing everything in his diabolical bag of magic tricks to avoid

being exposed. When he can, he even finds ways to turn it around to attack YOU and intimidate you and back you into a corner to further silence you—even more than you've already been silenced. The enemy clearly doesn't want this video to get out there, but I can promise you it will get posted.

Silence is Not an Option

I am not going to be intimidated into silence by anyone, not in the natural realm, and not in the spiritual realm. We are going to stand firm as a church. We're going to preach as a church. We are going to gather as a church. We are going to love as a church. And we're going to blow the trumpet, and blow the trumpet, and blow the trumpet, because while we're warning His people, the Lord is getting ready to blow another trumpet! We've got to get ready for Jesus to come again. So no one is going to silence me, no matter how many articles they write, how many threats they make. It just doesn't matter. I'll recraft my phraseology if need be and I'll apologize when the Holy Spirit leads me to, but I won't be silenced.

God doesn't call a watchman to timidly and shyly stand up at the top of this huge gathering spot and look out over the mountains to say softly, *"ladies and gentlemen, I certainly don't want to offend you, and I know most of you are going to have to run to your safe space when I'm done saying this, but I just want to remind you that the word of the LORD said unto me that you shouldn't worry because all things are going to be well in the end. Every day really is a Friday. God is always gonna bless you, and you're never gonna have any problems. You won't even have a headache, so relax."* I don't think so. God didn't call me to toot on the trumpet, He called me to BLOW it!

No Blood on My Hands

At the end of Ezekiel 33:4, the Lord says that if the sword comes and takes the watchman away, his blood and the blood of those he was to protect, would be upon his head. The Lord holds the watchmen responsible for ALL on his watch. So why am I going to speak now or forever hold my peace? Because your blood isn't going to be on my hands. The blood of the folks who look to me as their pastor or evangelist is not going to be on my hands. The blood of this nation is not going to be on my hands. God makes it clear that it will be upon the hearer if they hear the trumpet but don't properly respond. If you answer the call of the watchman that is on each of us, and your hearers don't heed your warnings, that's on them, not on you. But watch what He says in verse 5:

He heard the sound of the trumpet, and took not warning; his blood shall be upon him. But he that taketh warning shall deliver his soul.

~ *Ezekiel 33:5*

So in the context of this verse, you have two very important men. You have the watchman warning the people, and then you have the man that heard the warning and responded quickly to protect his family from the approaching enemy. In this context, the Bible says that when you warn the people, when you blow the trumpet, when you sound the alarm in Zion, their response is not your responsibility.

When I learned that in the ministry, it was like taking off the training wheels. It made things so much easier for me when I recognized that some plant and some water, but it's God, not Greg, who provides the increase, or—in this case—the way to overcome the attacking enemy. I realized that all I have to do is take the seed of the Word of God and just start scattering it all over the place and the seed will do the work. I don't have to manipulate. I don't have to beg, borrow, or steal. My only responsibility as a watchman is to give you the message, and your response is not on me. It's your responsibility to respond. You can enjoy the message, or you can hate the message. You can get to a place where you receive the message, or you despise the message. But once I give you the message, I've done my job. Now, if you want to receive the message and make full sense of it, I'll disciple you through it and I'll love you through it. I'll help you understand the message and we'll move forward together as we grow.

The Great Commission

I think one of the great problems in the local church is that we talk about folks getting saved, but we seldom ever disciple the people. People come to church and they get saved and they get baptized and they get born again, but they go up like a rocket and come down like a meteorite.

They don't stay with it because they don't get discipled through the message they received. That's too big a subject to fully expose in this book, but don't read this without realizing we're called not only to preach the Gospel, but we're also called to disciple those that receive it. We must teach them to obey all things whatsoever Jesus commanded, just as we read in the Great Commission as recorded in Mark 16 and Matthew 28.

Go ye therefore, and teach all nations, baptizing them in the name of the Father, and of the Son, and of the Holy Ghost: Teaching them to observe all things whatsoever I have commanded you: and, lo, I am with you always, even unto the end of the world. Amen.
~Jesus

Matthew 28:19-20

Metaphor of the Mailman

Imagine if tomorrow the mailman comes to your house and delivers a letter that is filled with vile curses and threats and angry, ridiculous, assorted nonsense. If you read that letter, you'd be rightly upset. So, imagine if the next day, you went out to wait for the mailman and when he rolled up to put junk in your mailbox, you said, *"let me tell you something, Mr. mailman. Let me tell you something Bucko. I don't care about your wrong-sided Jeep. Who do you think you are, driving up in my driveway bringing me a letter like that? You low down, sorry, good for nothing blankety-blank... I can't believe you're a government worker and I don't appreciate what that letter said!"*

That mailman is going to look at you like you have lost your mind, because he did not write the letter. He only delivered it to you and what you do with it is on you, not on him. So like Paw Paw used to say, you may not like the message, but don't you shoot the messenger. All he's doing is opening up your mailbox from his wrong-sided jeep and just sticking it in there. It's up to you what you do with it. But all this meek and mild, sweet, kind, compassionate, non-offensive, politically correct baby-Jesus stuff that we're hearing is an affront to God. They didn't kill Jesus because of what He did, they killed Jesus because of what He said, and He spoke a message that infuriated the enemy.

17

What Would Jesus Do?

The other day someone left a comment for me saying, "I've watched that angry video of yours and I just want to know one thing... what would Jesus do?" I rarely respond to those comments, but sometimes it's worth the price of admission. If you're going to ask me, "What would Jesus do?" I happen to read the Bible and I can easily tell you what Jesus DID. When it came to religion and politics, I know exactly what He did. All true Bible readers do. So don't ask "what would Jesus do" to accuse someone unless you know what He actually did in that context.

Most Bible readers know that Jesus sat down one day outside of the church building, patiently braided a whip, and then walked into the temple to turn the place upside down. Yes, we're talking about little meek and mild, all-forgiving baby Jesus, all grown up but still just a baby. Some try to say he just walked in as a show of force but didn't actually use the whip in anger. If you believe that, you ought to sue your brain for non-support. He whipped those people and all their animals right out of the church. Now I'm not advocating pastoral abuse, praise God, but don't ask me "what would Jesus do" in the context of a situation if you don't know what Jesus really did.

Jesus Said WHAT?
Jesus got sick of some of the stuff going on in the church, so He drove out the ones doing it. Many folks like to say, "I love the

Olivet Discourse... Matthew chapter 24 is such a beautifully deep and thoughtful passage." But you can't understand Matthew 24 without first understanding Matthew 23. It's the strongest most scathing sermon that ever fell from the lips of a human being, ever. Jesus was like, "you fools, you hypocrites, you serpents, you blind guides, you generation of vipers, you bunch of devils, you're like dead men's bones... "how can you escape the damnation of hell?" And that was to a crowd of religious leaders.

That's the sort of thing Jesus would do if He were here today, and those people were like saints compared to what we're witnessing in the Christendom today. John the Baptist wasn't the only man of God in the New Testament to throw down on lawless hypocrites. He simply prepared the way. When Jesus unloaded his Gospel gun, the religious hypocrites were always his target. On this day, everyone in ear shot was sitting there, like, "WHAT did he just say?" Yes, he said it. I'm all for the forgiveness of God, and I know I need it as much as anyone, but you'd better know we're living in the days of judgment right now. We have so vilified and watered down the holiness of God that anything goes. It's all "que sera, sera" in the church, and that isn't what the Bible teaches. It's the lukewarm stuff that turns the Lord's stomach. The word of God tells us to raise up a holy army of God's people to push back against the tidal wave of this wicked culture. Will we?

If I don't Blow the Trumpet?

But if the watchman see the sword come, and blow not the trumpet, and the people be not warned; if the sword come, and take any person from among them, he is taken away in his iniquity; but his blood will I require at the watchman's hand.

~ Ezekiel 33:6

In the context of verse six, the watchman sees the sword coming. He sees the advancing enemy. He sees the judgment of God, but he doesn't blow the trumpet. Why? Because he's afraid he'll offend someone. He's afraid someone is going to leave the church. He's afraid someone is going to get upset and unfriend him on Facebook, or shun him in public, so he doesn't blow the trumpet. Afterall, you know, he still has to go to a family reunion with these people and he doesn't want politics and religion to make them uncomfortable. I'm counting on it! We need to get uncomfortable about such complacency. But notice, if the watchman doesn't blow the trumpet and the people are not warned, if the sword comes and takes any person—ANY person—from among them, he is taken away in his iniquity. But his blood will be on the watchman's hands, says the Lord. If there's something that should prompt a "Not on my watch," there it is. There are no survivors in this part of the prophecy.

Truth in Love

I love everybody enough to tell you the truth, and I hope you do too, because the Bible says to speak the truth in love. It doesn't say to speak love at the expense of the truth. That's a critical distinction that is dismissed far too often in the Church. If it's truth, it's loving. But if it's all love and no truth, it's actually a form of hate, because it would be built on untruths. A true heart loves enough to tell the truth even if it hurts. And that's why the truth will make you free. The Lord said that a man may die because of his sin, and every bucket sits on its own bottom, so I don't see him surviving such an attack with no defenses.

When the enemy strikes, if the trumpet doesn't blast to alert the people, the person that is going to be held responsible for their deaths before God is the watchman. Why? Because he didn't do what God told him to do. It's really quite simple, isn't it? And please hear my heart here, pastors and preachers and priests are not the only ones who are called to be watchmen. Are you willing to be a watchman where you are? Are you willing to warn your family of the impending persecution and judgment of God? Are you willing to stand against the tidal wave of this iniquitous culture that we are living in, this rebellious day of people that have been turned over to a reprobate mind? You can argue with them. You can try but you'll just get frustrated, angry, and demoralized. We are living in days where you are on one side or the other. And phooey on this idea that you're either Republican or a Democrat. When it comes to an election, you'd better be a Christian first and a Christian last.

Non-Negotiables

The Bible is clear about our requirement to follow the Judeo-Christian moral code, which is the foundation of our Constitution. And the 1st Amendment guarantees our right to practice our faith unencumbered, without restrictions. We have the law of the land and all righteousness on our side. All we have to do is stand up and publicly speak out and start calling all Christians to vote the Bible before it's too late. 25 million Evangelicals aren't even registered to vote? Come on pastors! If I've done my job as a watchman, I won't have to tell you who to vote for. You've got enough sense to know who to vote for because there are things going on that we the church cannot possibly support. There is stuff we simply can't stand for and stuff we can no longer put up with. According to the word of God, there are non-negotiables. There are some issues that we can disagree on and still be friends. But there are a few issues that—if we disagree—we'd have to part ways, because the Bible says to mark them, avoid them, and have no company with them (1 Corinthians 5:11).

Even among friends, there are some folks that don't want to be in a bold living church. There are some folks that can't handle the journey. There are some folks that aren't built for the trip, and that's okay. But the rest of us should get bolder than ever before.

God is Ticked Off

I don't want people's blood to be on my hands. I don't ever want the Holy Spirit to say, "I want you to say this" and then I go to bed beating myself up for not saying it. If I love people, I'm going to say it. Speak now or forever hold your peace. Then notice in verse seven:

So thou, O son of man, I have set thee a watchman unto the house of Israel; therefore thou shalt hear the word at my mouth, and warn them from me.

~ Ezekiel 33:7

We understand contextually who God was speaking to and why he was speaking, but the Bible is a book of application. When a nation is in distress, it needs watchmen whether it's Israel or America or wherever it is. He said, "therefore, thou shalt hear the word at my mouth." Not the word of man, not the word of social media, not the word of any other source. The word of God from His mouth, and He tells us to "warn them from me." Warn them from me. Well, that's not a verse or a phrase or a sentence that gets preached a whole lot. Why am I blowing the trumpet? Because God is ticked off. Because God isn't happy with us.

You can't have a nation that swims in as much violence and perversion as we have and imagine God is okay with it. But nothing distresses the heart of our Savior more than the evil and deception we're seeing on so many levels these days, and the fact that we're allowing it all to happen, on our watch. That is the curse of the lukewarm church in America. God said, you get hot or you get cold, but don't you be in the middle or I'll spew you out of my mouth. (Revelation 3:16) He said to me, I want you to "warn them from me." I believe He's saying that to you too.

When I say unto the wicked, O wicked man, thou shalt surely die; if thou dost not speak to warn the wicked from his way, that wicked man shall die in his iniquity; but his blood will I require at thine hand.

~ Ezekiel 33:8

In verse eight the Bible says, "When I say unto the wicked, O wicked man, thou shalt surely die." We see that God is patient by mere fact that He warns us despite our wickedness, but even God's patience wears out in the face of rebellion and iniquity. God said, if you'll do your job, if you'll warn the nation, if you'll warn the church, if you'll warn your family, if you'll warn your kids, if you'll warn the people, if you'll just do it.

God said, if you'll do your job you can walk away from every conflict and dust your feet off and sleep good at night, because you said what was supposed to be said. But if God tells you to say it, and you don't, I hope food doesn't taste good to you and you don't sleep a wink for the next six months. I want you to finish this book with a holy uncomfortability that you're not happy where you are in your walk with God.

I'm not happy where I am. I want to read more, pray more, preach more, win more, love more, forgive more. Listen, I want to do more for the glory of God in 2020 and beyond. I don't care how terrible and "fall down the steps" 2020 has been. I want to see revival in my own life, and in my church, and in my nation, and all around the globe. That's what I want to see.

Do it Now

I know this much. In the context of Ezekiel 33 I'm going to deliver my soul. I'm going to say my peace. I won't go silent on my watch. I'm going to keep on sounding the trumpet and shouting, "the Redcoats are coming, The Redcoats are coming" because Jesus is coming, Jesus is coming. I'm going to keep on beating the drum and I'll just keep on stirring them up. I don't mind walking into a

162

hornet's nest even though I'm allergic to stings. So I compel you to say the same, especially you men. You'd better speak now or forever hold your peace. Don't think you can start speaking in five years or so.

To the pastors who closed down their churches for 25 weeks and are patting yourselves on your backs for finally opening up, you've got to recognize that you have some serious ground to make up, and great damage will be done to the body that could have been avoided. You should have kept your church open the whole time. That's what you should have done, and you know it. Deep inside I know you know it. What are you going to do about those 25 weeks you should have been blowing the trumpet? The people that needed a hope center in a desperate time but found no Church to help them? I hope you'll get your people caught up as soon as possible. Everything truly is at stake, so don't for one-minute think that's hyperbole. In these final days, living churches with effective watchmen are standing on the Gospel and the principles of the Word of God every single day. Be part of a living church for the sake of the Church. There can be no other agenda in these days. It's the call of Christ to feed and protect His Church with the Word of God. Speak the words of Jesus when He proclaimed the beginning of His mission and make them your own.

"The Spirit of the Lord is upon me, because he hath anointed me to preach the Gospel to the poor; he hath sent me to heal the brokenhearted, to preach deliverance to the captives, and recovering of sight to the blind, to set at liberty them that are bruised" ~ Jesus (reading from Isaiah)

~ Luke 4:18

Not for Everyone

It is time to blow the trumpet Church! Some of the people that are in your closest circle are good people, but they're not going to be able to make the journey through the spiritual war at hand. They're not going to be able to make the next step, and that's okay. Because where the Lord is leading us isn't for everybody. It should be, but it's not. There are some things you can't put back in the box. You just can't. The reason I'm so passionate and adamant about the "speak now or forever hold your peace" message, wasn't intended to be a means to Facebook notoriety. In 2015 I wasn't looking for blue check marks or clicks or likes or TikTok, Twitter, or Instagram. It just wasn't part of the plan. But it happened, right?

I can't go back now—not that I would—and I can't put it back in the box. Things have been said, things have happened, and God promoted our church to an international platform and has connected us with so many of the most influential people in the body of Christ that it's hard to believe sometimes. We never could have imagined in our little Nashville hillbilly sense that we'd be hosting the move of the Holy Spirit in this way. And I'm not teasing our people... I call myself a hillbilly because I am in fact a hillbilly, born and bred in the hills of Middle Tennessee. I don't know why God has chosen to do what he's doing with us. But we can't go back from this, and I pray that everyone reading this book is ready to sound the trumpet right there where you are or join us where we are. The Lord is doing something you won't want to miss.

Here We Are

Here we are together, meeting in this book or at Global Vision, live or online, brother to brother all loving each other. Thousands of us. And I'm honored you've taken the time to read what the Lord is speaking to me. I can't take back all the controversy I've stirred in the past, and I can't take back the brokenness, nor would I. And I can't take back the media attacks or the fact that the left hates us, mostly because of me. I can't take back the fact that we are the most polarizing church in this community.

You either really like us or you can't stand us, and when I walk into a store, I know which is which. I can't help that. I can't put it back into the box. So the only thing my mind can reconcile is—since we can't go back with it—we might as well just go forward with it. If it's truth, and we can't undo it, we might as well just walk in it for the reality that it is and let God do what God wants to do with it. It's time to proclaim the Gospel like never before, and enforce its purpose and preeminence, come what may, in Jesus' name.

Closing Prayer

Please pray this short prayer with me. Father, today we ask that Your power and anointing would fall on us. We realize we don't have time to get courageous later. It's past time for us to be courageous. Your Word says the wicked flee when no man pursues, but the righteous are bold as a lion. We have nothing to be afraid of. We are saved by the grace of God from the top of our head to the soles of our feet. We're indwelt by the power of the Holy Spirit, we have this book called The Bible, we are the local church, the pillar and the ground of the truth, and hell itself and the gates thereof cannot come against us and prevail. And yet some want to be timid? Forgive us Lord. We want to talk about what we would have done. Want to talk about what we'll get around to. Break that Lord. We know we've got to do it now, Lord Jesus. If we're going to win our kids to Christ, in spirit and in truth, we know we've got to do it now. If we're going to watch you restore our lives, we got to do it now. If we're going to see you move, we've got to do it now. Speak now Lord. Or may we forever hold our peace. So God, I pray for a spirit of courage for me and all who read this prayer. I ask for the spirit of the bold lion within us to walk right into the face of adversity, to walk into the fiery furnace, to walk to the guillotine, to walk to the prison cell, if that's where You lead us. May You give us a boldness that is so supernatural that we don't even understand it ourselves. You told me not to worry about what to say and not to premeditate what to say but just to open my mouth and you will fill it. Let the redeemed of the Lord say so, whom the Lord has redeemed out of the hand of the enemy, give us a heart to climb the steps of the watchtower and blow the trumpet. If they hear it, praise God. If they reject it, so be it. There are a lot of things I'm not. And there are a lot of things I'll never be, and the world can say what they will and identify us any way they choose to. But Father, I ask that one thing you will never call me is a coward... ever. So give me a passion to speak the truth of your Word boldly and lovingly, but Biblically true. In Jesus' holy name, amen.

CONCLUSION

One of the things that I admire most about the ministry of Jesus Christ was how He had the ability to state a bold cutting truth and then simply walk away. Jesus was the original person of the mic drop moment. He did not defend His statements. On many occasions He did not even define his statements. He was so clear and transparent, that His words and His passion rallied people behind His cause, building a massive and influential following along the way.

We must remind ourselves that Jesus was not crucified because of what He *did*, but rather for what He *said*. The religious and political leaders of His day couldn't stand the fact that He boldly and plainly called things for what they were. He didn't play games when it came to the truth. The tactics of Jesus were simple; say what needs to be said and walk out of the room.

I recognize that much of this book hasn't been your average reading material. While compiling the material, the very design and desire of my heart was to be real, raw, and authentic in everything that was said. I didn't write this book to stand as a theological treatise in any way. Its sole purpose is to encourage people's hearts to seek more of the will and the word of God in these last days. I'm convinced that most people aren't looking for something that is completely polished. They're looking for something that is completely honest!

It's time for the masks to come off, and I mean that literally and figuratively. It's also high time for the gloves to come off. We're not shadow boxing anymore. This is a UFC takedown straight to the mat. I realize that some of you picked up this book out of sheer curiosity, because much of what I do in the public arena is shrouded in controversy. I do hope however that what you have read has been a timely message and a great help. If nothing else, I pray it sparks a brighter fire in your curiosity.

Because of the ongoing dismantling of our nation's fundamental beliefs, it is imperative that we speak more loudly and focus more of our attention on the political arena. But in the midst of it all, we must keep our focus on Jesus Christ. If I have the ability to encourage you to be bold and yet do not point you to the Gospel of Jesus Christ, I have failed. The Bible says that whosoever shall call upon the name of the Lord shall be saved. If you have never turned to the Lord Jesus Christ in faith, I'm not merely asking you to be an activist, I am imploring you to repent and believe the Gospel. Don't try to save the country while letting your own soul go to hell.

I don't know what the future holds, but I certainly know who holds the future. The beauty about tomorrow is in the fact that God has already been there, and He tells us not to fret. We are not to be filled with a spirit of fear. Ever. As you close this book and determine what to take away from it, I want to encourage you with undeniable and foundational facts that will never change. These are *constants* in a world of confusion. No matter what we face and no matter how everything turns out, these truths will never perish.

1. The Bible will still be the Word of God.
2. The Lord will still be upon His throne.
3. Jesus is still coming back.
4. Revival is still very much possible.

I have no idea what the Lord is going to do with this book. And as beautiful and helpful as it would be for our cause, I'm not at all concerned about achieving bestseller status. If He decides to do that, praise God. What I do know is that when I read what I've written, it strikes me to the core. I find myself under conviction and tearing up even though I know what is coming. That's truly powerful for me, so I pray this book has the same impact on you!

Made in the USA
Monee, IL
05 October 2020

44058415R00104